Among the Aspen

AMONG THE ASPEN

Northwoods Grouse and Woodcock Hunting

MARK PARMAN

THE UNIVERSITY OF WISCONSIN PRESS

The University of Wisconsin Press
1930 Monroe Street, 3rd Floor
Madison, Wisconsin 537112059
uwpress.wisc.edu

3 Henrietta Street, Covent Garden
London WCE8LU, United Kingdom
eurospanbookstore.com

Printed in the United States of America

This book may be available in a digital edition.

Library of Congress Cataloging-in-Publication Data

Names: Parman, Mark, author.
Title: Among the aspen: northwoods grouse and woodcock hunting / Mark Parman.
Description: Madison, Wisconsin: The University of Wisconsin Press, [2018]
Identifiers: LCCN 2017044545 | ISBN 9780299317508 (cloth: alk. paper)
Subjects: LCSH: Parman, Mark. | Grouse shooting—Wisconsin—Anecdotes.
| Woodcock shooting—Wisconsin—Anecdotes. | Bird dogs—Anecdotes.
Classification: LCC SK325. G7 P268 2018 | DDC 799. 2/463—dc23
LC record available at https://lccn.loc.gov/2017044545

As always,

to
SUSAN

He usually does not own the deed, but in a strange way he possesses a grouse covert as he is possessed by it, holding special title to that particular corner of this earth, a carry-over from the age when man discovered wild land and made it his.

GEORGE BIRD EVANS

No wealth can buy the requisite leisure, freedom, and independence, which are the capital in this profession.

HENRY DAVID THOREAU

Contents

EAST

WEST

Among the Aspen

Introduction

Among the Aspen

When Norman Maclean was shopping around the manuscript for his novel *A River Runs Through It*, one editor returned it with a rejection note saying, "These stories have trees in them." Like Maclean's stories, my essays have trees in them as well, for this is where ruffed grouse and woodcock live and where upland hunters must go to pursue them. The first place I look is an aspen cutting, for no other tree appeals to grouse and woodcock like *Populus tremuloides*, the quaking aspen.

Besides trees, this book has stories in it, a lot of stories, which apparently is not what most hunting editors want. They tell me stories don't sell very well these days. Send us something how-to or where-to, and we'll take a look. If you want to read a how-to hunt grouse book, there are some excellent choices: Dennis Walrod's *Grouse Hunter's Guide* or Don Johnson's *Grouse & Woodcock: A Gunner's Guide*. Better yet, find a mentor and tag along, or simply find some aspen, start walking, and learn by trial and error because in many ways it's not a complicated sport. I bungled along like that for some time, and still do on occasion.

These essays are grounded in my coverts, the secret places I and my dogs hunt. I also use the term "cover" but when doing so refer to vegetation: the trees, brush, and thickets ruffed grouse and woodcock haunt. In northern Wisconsin, cover could mean tag alders, balsam fir or blackberry canes, and, of course, aspen.

To most people, "covert" means hidden, clandestine, or undercover. The word conjures up the secret operations of the CIA or the KGB. But to a grouse hunter, a covert is a noun, not an adjective, a place where game lurks and finds shelter. Most grouse and woodcock hunters are reluctant to reveal where their coverts are and go to great lengths to keep them secret. Don't even ask. In fact, I changed many of the names of mine in the following chapters—for obvious reasons to any grouse and woodcock hunter. Some secrets must remain.

For twenty-five years, I've been discovering and stringing together a line of coverts across north-central Wisconsin. If you're a veteran grouse hunter, you might have a file of marked-up and tattered maps of your coverts or at least a mental one. If you're new to grouse and woodcock hunting, you should start one immediately if you have not yet done so.

I dream of these places, at night and sometimes during the day. On this steamy August afternoon when the air has the clarity of a dishrag, I'm thinking of a place in northern Lincoln County in October, where from high on a ridge I can see the burning red of the sugar maples and the gold of aspen across the waves of multiple ridges. The few wispy clouds overhead trace setter tails across the pure blue, while down in the lowland, the dog's white tail swishes and flags through tangled cover. This daydream helps me endure the stagnant green of an August afternoon.

Although nearly every one of my coverts lies on public ground, I claim them as my own even though they are open and free to anyone who would care to roam there, including nonhunters. Part of my ownership arises from naming them, usually after something notable occurring there, like the Bermuda Triangle, where freak accidents and unusual mishaps hang in the air. In these places, the narrative of our lives weaves itself into the landscape, our acts inflecting the land we walk upon. I name coverts for an object or natural feature, like '53

Ford, named after the old pickup abandoned and rusting quietly along a logging road. The side panels and doors riddled with bullet holes and peppered with #8 shot attest to the fact this covert is shared ground and my property and naming rights here are clearly in question. Since possession is said to be 90 percent of ownership, I return often to my favorite coverts to assert my title. I need to stake "my" claim—that, and I might shoot a bird or two along the way.

I live and hunt in northern Wisconsin, in a place geologists refer to as the northern or Lake Superior highlands. Most of my hunting is confined to four or five counties in north-central Wisconsin. Eons ago, this land was mountainous, like the Rockies or Alps, but snow and rain, wind and streams—and all that geologic time—eroded the once lofty mountains, gradually wearing them down to what's left today, a rolling and forested upland, punctuated by lakes and ridges and drained by fast, clear rivers. The highest point in the state is less than two thousand feet in elevation. From where I live, this upland area stretches all the way north through Ontario to Hudson Bay in Canada. Locals call this place the Northwoods, and people from down south, below Highway 29, often refer to it as Up North.

Northwoods sums up this place. Its northern climate features relatively cool summers, particularly around Lake Superior. You can wear blue jeans and flannel the entire summer in Duluth. I've heard people say summer is just three months of bad skiing or bad sledding (snowmobiling). Winters here can be brutal, and they do drive people south to places like Florida and Arizona. That's why the Packers are beloved in those Sun Belt states. I have cross-country skied on Easter too many times to remember, and even though the ruffed grouse season lasts until the end of January, winter and deep snow effectively end it sometimes in early November, occasionally before all the woodcock have escaped to their warmer winter quarters in the Deep South.

No tree dominates this landscape like the white pine, a tree that has little value to grouse and woodcock hunters other than its beauty, which to me is important. When I hunt, I'm after birds and stories,

Pushing through prime aspen cover, where it's like shooting in a phone booth. (Susan Parman)

but these days I also go hunting for beauty. Fewer than two hundred years ago, this upland was covered with virgin white pine until they were razed by greed and insolence, the logging companies treating the vast forest like a cornfield. The board feet that went downstream to the cities in the South must have been staggering, as were the profits. Lumberjacks felled these cloud-scraping trees with two-man crosscut saws, which is how tough guys did it before chain saws. It must have been something to walk beneath these giants and sight up their trunks, and even the most flint-hearted Swede or Finnish logger must have felt some awe underneath these pines. Nevertheless, most grouse hunters ignore the white pine other than as scenery, since it offers little by way of habitat or food to ruffed grouse and woodcock.

After the great white pine were decimated, colonizing species like aspen moved in around the stumps. Aspen—which hunters commonly refer to as popple—is the tree dominating most of my stories. It's the most important tree to a bird hunter, since grouse and woodcock find food and shelter from the aspen. Both birds are usually found within shooting distance of aspen, although that is not a hard-and-fast rule, especially when considering woodcock. Given that, I don't pass by an aspen cutting without at least a cursory run through it.

Aspen looks similar to birch, with its whitish-gray bark, but regrettably it doesn't have the papery bark hanging in sheets from larger trees, for that would be much more literary. I could exploit a metaphor about stories written on the birchbark paper fluttering in the wind, but birch isn't used to make paper. On the other hand, popple happens to be a most important tree for the paper industry in the Northwoods, so these stories may ultimately be printed on aspen after all.

The popple is a common tree. It's not celebrated in literature, like the birch, the white pine, the oak, or the elm. It does glow briefly in October, its leaves turning golden and reminding me of coins, and it makes a clear and bright paneling. It grows in vast clumps of clones and sends up root suckers from a parent tree. Individual popple trees may live only thirty or fifty years, but the root system is long lived, and some systems in the Rockies are thousands of years old. Measured by the roots, some popple colonies are the oldest trees in the Northwoods, older even than the most massive white pine.

Initially the root suckers come up, after clear-cutting or fire, as thick as blackberry canes, which is why it shelters grouse and wood-cock so effectively. Stem densities of five thousand to eight thousand per acre are ideal for grouse. A hunter must fight through cover with tree density this heavy, as do other predators, like goshawks, owls, fox, and coyote. Ruffed grouse also happen to feed on the popple buds, particularly in winter when it is their main food. You can often find grouse on a winter afternoon as the weak January sun is setting, perching in mature popple, picking the buds, and filling their crops. The woodcock does not eat popple buds or catkins, preferring a diet of worms.

After the virgin white pine were cut, farmers followed the loggers, and some of the loggers took up farming because they wanted to stay in the Northwoods, but this isn't the ideal place to farm. In most places, only a thin layer of topsoil is scattered over the granite below, and it's not uncommon to see frosts in both June and August, al-though there are places, like the fertile river valleys, where farming still thrives. Where it didn't, the fields have reverted back to woods. Like the virgin stumps left rotting in the woods, I happen across rusting barbwire fences and old stone barn foundations, evidence of an attempt at farming. When the owners went belly up, they picked up, left their land, and moved on. Much of this forfeited land is what we hunt today, bought and paid for by the Pittman-Robertson Act, one of the finest pieces of legislation Congress ever enacted. Vacant, and tax delinquent in some cases, the land was bought or reverted back to the government and now forms the basis of the millions of acres of public land in Wisconsin.

The pastures and farm fields grew back into mostly aspen stands. The logging industry continues to cut much of this industrial forest, perpetuating the brushy second growth. With all of this new wood, biologists tell us upland bird numbers here are conceivably at historic highs. There are more grouse here than there were two hundred years ago, they say, and Wisconsin has arguably the highest bird numbers of any state, although Minnesota or Michigan could justifiably dispute this claim.

It's a good place for a grouse or woodcock hunter to live. I have no reason to complain.

Fergus and Jenkins, my two English setters, appear in the following essays and need introducing. Fergus, a blue belton of seventy pounds, was born in 2009. He looks like one of George Bird Evans's Old Hemlock setters. We're still arguing whether we named Fergus after Jim or Charles. Susan says he's named after Jim Fergus, author of *A Hunter's Road* and *One Thousand White Women*; I say he's named after Charles Fergus, author of *The Upland Equation* and *A Rough-Shooting Dog*. All these books are worth reading.

Jenkins, a tricolor of sixty pounds, was born in 2012. When a high school friend heard we had put money down on a second setter, he suggested we call the new pup Jenkins. It took me a few moments to get the Ferguson Jenkins reference to the former Chicago Cubs Hall of Fame pitcher. On our high school baseball team, my friend pitched and I caught, and together we idolized Fergie, who won games even though he rarely had any hitting behind him, the Cubs in the 1970s having difficulty scoring runs.

Fergus, who is gentle and mannerly, is clearly above Jenkins in our pack order. Fergus would rather hunt than do any other thing—except possibly eat. Jenkins worships Fergus. Sometimes we feel Jenkins cares more for Fergus than us, and whenever I hunt the two together, I can always count on Jenkins to find Fergus—who ranges out farther than Jenkins—when I've lost Fergus on a faraway point. Jenkins is the more nervous of the two, the first to bark, and standoffish when he meets strangers for the first time. He also possesses an exuberance that is contagious. He routinely jumps for joy, an antic that never ceases to put a smile on my face. Both dogs have strong prey drives, and yet they're loving house dogs who like nothing better than snuggling on the sofa or in bed. Much of this was written with one or the other curled up between my outstretched legs on the ottoman.

Both my setters hunt grouse and woodcock exclusively. Other than one three-day trip to southwest Iowa to hunt pheasants and quail, they have hunted only in northern Wisconsin. I started both as puppies on woodcock and then moved them on to ruffed grouse, and we thankfully live in a place abundant with wild birds. I don't consider myself an expert trainer by any stretch, and really only enforce two commands—*Come* and *Whoa*. Any blame for the faults of my dogs should be laid at my door. They hunt four to five days a week during the season, which means they have had ample opportunities to learn the ways and habits of grouse and woodcock, and this, I believe, is the best method for making a good grouse or woodcock dog. I continually remind them they are lucky dogs.

I never set out to hunt behind setters; this just happened. Years ago, our first setter, Ox, was a chance acquisition. But like many others who hunt setters, we fell in love with their gentle bearing combined with their ability in the woods. Other grouse and woodcock hunters have found other breeds to suit their tastes and temperaments, which is as it should be. I quickly learned pointing dogs suited my style of meandering around, thinking about whatever crosses my mind and not paying the dog much mind until it starts to make game. If I hunted pheasants in Iowa or quail in Arizona, it's likely I would hunt a different breed. At any rate, many dog breeds are capable of hunting grouse and woodcock successfully as well as many different ways to hunt them. Although I can't conceive of bird hunting without a dog, many hunters do and have success.

Someday, when my legs can no longer keep pace with my setters, a day I pray is a long time coming, I will get a cocker spaniel—at least

I tell myself this—and I would try to keep the little flusher close and potter along behind its short legs. Whatever dog I own then, however, I hope to keep following it, perhaps through some of the very coverts I've written about here, until I can no longer walk in the grouse woods among the aspen. That is how I would like my story to end.

The Wilderness Covert

Up on this ridge, the red oaks stand tall, colossal trees with spreading crowns. It's a dark old forest that looks as though it hasn't been cut in years. I didn't expect to see any birds here, but you never know. Jenkins extended his range underneath the widely spaced old trees. This damp October day the overcast sky sagged down on us, so I was glad to be in these older, more open woods.

This fall the mast hung heavy on the oaks, and white-tailed deer will feed on this windfall and grow fat in hopes of making it through the long winter. Grouse, too, will eat the nutritious and meaty acorns, but, with little of the brushy cover they favor under the oaks, they probably won't risk exposing themselves. Still, I reminded myself to be ready and not be thunderstruck by a wild flushing grouse if Jenkins happened to be working the other side of the trail. I kept my shotgun ready at port arms.

I was hunting in a national forest semiprimitive area, which I call the Wilderness Covert, even though by no stretch is it a primeval wilderness. The woods have been logged, maybe once or twice in the last century, so it's not virgin timber, and there's an old dam downstream leftover from the first logging. A farmer or two may also have tried to cultivate the level ground down along the river or up on the ridges, but the thin soil, rocks, and short growing season almost certainly forced them out. If you look close enough, you might find evidence of their tenure, an old barbwire fence or a moss-covered granite foundation. Standing still, I could hear a vehicle rattling down the gravel road behind me and an occasional jet droned overhead. From the ruts in the softer sections of trail, it was obvious, despite the signs prohibiting motorized vehicles, an ATV occasionally churned through this supposedly motorless area.

Humans have used and still use this land. We have left and continue to leave our mark. This place, however, is one of the wildest spots in Wisconsin, if we define this by lack of human activity and disturbance, and, as far as my coverts go, it feels more like a wilderness than any other.

It had been nearly ten years since I hunted the Wilderness Covert, and I came to renew my sense of the place. This is not a great place to hunt grouse, since the cover is mostly old woods and the US Forest Service is not known for "cutting hard." In northern Wisconsin, the counties cut their forest much harder and as such provide better habitat for species dependent on young forest, like grouse and woodcock. Productive upland cover, nevertheless, is often claustrophobic and restricting. You must fight your way through it. I can find it oppressive, especially on a damp, gray day such as this. So on occasion I hunt places like the Wilderness with open, expansive views, yet significantly fewer birds. It's a trade-off—better scenery, fewer birds—but it's a fair trade.

If we put up any grouse, it will probably be down along the river where the tag alders and other nameless brush grew, in the thick and suffocating cover. If one flushes down there, I tell myself to shoot it before it crosses the river. Fifteen years ago, I was hunting with a friend and his Chesapeake Bay retriever, a dog that would swim across an icy lake to fetch a downed bird, so we didn't hesitate to shoot out over the river. Jenkins only likes to get his toes wet, however. He's not swimming after a downed bird, so if one goes that way I will have to let it go.

My friend has since moved and sold his land and cabin down the road, which is one of the reasons that I haven't hunted this "semi-primitive area" for so long. We had a duck blind down on a bend in the river and spent many opening mornings hunkered there, shotguns at the ready in the growing daylight. Once we had tundra swans drop into our decoys, along with the usual Canada geese, mallards, teal, and the occasional diver duck. The wood ducks would mostly scream up and down the river, offering pass shooting.

Once, the waterfowl opener was warm, humid, and mosquito filled, and as the sky started to lighten, a front moved in from the northwest with a rush of wind, thunder, and lightning. The Canadian front also brought in the ducks, which we could see dropping into the decoys between the flashes of lightning. It was like shooting in the strobing light of a disco, the world jumpy and jerky, illuminated in still-life frames. It was, and probably will remain, the most memorable day of waterfowling in my life. When the front had passed—the thunder growling on the eastern horizon and the light coming back—we picked up our ducks, only then realizing the danger we had been in sitting in a metal boat, holding lightning rods.

But there were also grouse down along the river, and we hunted them on the two-mile walk in and out, shooting them with the steel shot required for waterfowl. Any we shot, we would eat that evening, roasting them over an open fire under Orion and the Pleiades.

I was thinking about that long-ago duck hunt on the drive over, first on the state highway, then the county highway and onto the gravel roads of the national forest until we finally bumped our way a hundred yards down a two-track, parking next to sofa-sized boulders blocking the trail. It's marked as a nonmotorized trail, but it takes impediments like these to keep the motors out, and sometimes even that doesn't work. Without a motor, however, I would not be hunting this trail once again, since I drove forty miles to get here.

It took my senses awhile to get used to walking after driving. I had taken in little of nature on the drive over, the green world whizzing by at sixty miles an hour, each tree a blur. Only when we hit the gravel, halved our speed, and I had rolled the passenger window down so Jenkins could stick his head out did we get a fuller picture of where we were. Jenkins, I suspected, was taking in much more of the world with his nose than I was with my eyes. If only he could talk and describe the smells. It would take me more time to adjust, to lift the scales from my eyes so I could be fully present. Jenkins's entrance was immediate. He was there when he jumped out of the cab. I, on the other hand, needed to trade my indoor mind, the one stuck inside the cab looking at dials and gauges and listening to rock-and-roll, for my outdoor one.

As the trail dropped down off the ridge into the chasm cut by the river, Jenkins continued to zigzag up the ridge and down the slope toward the trail. On the lower slopes, the red oaks gave way to popple mixed with balsam fir and the occasional yellow birch and hemlock, which thrive in the shade of the north-facing grades. Unlike the typical popple cutting, it was dark beneath these trees, and it smelled of mold and rotting wood. The birch were old and dying, strips of bark hanging like beards from their thick trunks. They would make wonderful firewood, but they were even more impressive standing there alongside the trail, silently and slowly collapsing.

I had stopped to watch Jenkins scramble down the slope, dancing among the old trees and over the downed and rotting limbs. He was the more athletic of our dogs. He could skip through the woods like a deer, making it hard to keep up with him at times, though most times he worked close. Not only did he sense this world better than I; he moved through it much more gracefully and efficiently on his four legs. His long coat also protected him better than my brush pants.

While I was standing in the trail, admiring the way he wove among the trees and rocks, a grouse flushed from behind me. I pivoted at the sound—one I can hear in my dreams—as the bird barreled up the slope. Jenkins was plunging downslope, the bird angling left-to-right away from him and up the slope toward the red oaks. He stopped and watched it flush up the hill.

Tracking both sight and sound, I got my shotgun to my shoulder, and as the barrel passed through the bird, I pulled the trigger. But just then the bird banked behind a mature birch, the shot string tearing into the bark and sending up a shower of white confetti. The bird continued to beat upslope, unharmed.

I looked over at Jenkins—he was standing facing me with his front legs planted on a rock, head turned, looking where the bird had fled. Normally after the shot, he's off to search for the downed bird, but he knew this one would make the ridge top and keep flying over the other side. Like many of my thoughts, this one was in the clear for just a moment, there for the taking, before it disappeared over the horizon, perhaps to never again be encountered. We didn't follow up the bird, the steep slope making the decision for me.

So we moved on, the trail dropping down alongside the river. Here the river is squeezed in a narrow canyon, and the water lathers and foams over rocks. It's not much more than ten yards across to the other bank, hardly a river if size is what matters. My friend claimed a logging road used to cross the river here on the rocks. For a moment, I consider fording the river on the moss-covered rocks, but then realize Jenkins would never follow. I would no doubt fall into the cold water as well. A pair of wood ducks, both males, jet by low over the water, squealing as they head downstream to the slower, more open water behind the dam.

A bit beyond the ford, the trail dips to its lowest point, cutting through a dense clot of old tag alders. As I walk through the tags on the trail, two brown blurs flush out of the tag alders and across the river. Right on cue, like clockwork, I hear them more than see them, and even if I managed to drop one it would land in the swift water and be quickly swept downstream. They seem to know better than to flush south and up the ridge, in the direction where I could get a good shot.

They did so once. We had finished a morning sitting in our blind, and we had had success and were talking and joking about who hit what duck and who missed as we walked back to the truck, so we really were in no way thinking about upland birds when three grouse rocketed up the slope. We wasted four or five shells between the two of us on those birds, but we did have another story to joke about.

Has natural selection honed this local population? Only the birds flushing across the river survive; those who fly across the open trail and into the mature woods die and don't pass on their less fit genes. But if this were the case, then the population of ruffed grouse that fly up into trees when flushed or peck gravel in the ditch, even after a truck door has slammed, or sit tightly frozen in front of a pointing dog would long ago have been wiped out. Birds with these tendencies haven't learned to adapt to a predator armed with a shotgun. There seemed to be no shortage of these foolish birds—or my half-baked amateur theories of natural selection.

When I got to the spit that juts out into the river and leads to our old duck blind, I turned down it and fought through the dense aspen and alders that thin to marsh grass as the spit narrows and drops down to the water. Where the spit ended, rotting tops of logs stick a few inches above the water and march across to the other side. At one time, a railroad bridge spanned the river here, for the trains that pulled out the last of the virgin white pine, maple, oak, and hemlock. Out on the water, no evidence of the blind we carefully built so many years ago remained. Across the river, rocks rise precipitously from the shore. Some of the boulders are the size of small buildings—a one-room schoolhouse or a garage—and one rock is shaped like a giant ball. We called it the melon.

At the duck opener, the maples flamed on that northern shoreline, and I thought it was one of the most beautiful places on earth. Back in the city, I would wonder what it looked like as it passed through the seasons. What did it look like as the first snow fell or when it was thirty below? What did it look like as the hepatica and bloodroot bloomed? What did it sound like when the thrushes or whitethroats sang?

I took one long, last look into the water, searching for a scrap of wood or rotting piece of burlap, maybe an old rusty wire, but found nothing. If I had worn waders, I would have made my way out through the muck, ever mindful of the one deep hole, for a closer look. But I didn't, so I called Jenkins and pushed back through the brush toward the trail.

There are several ways to define wilderness. The classic definition of the 1964 Wilderness Act claims: "A wilderness, in contrast with those areas where man and his own works dominate the landscape, is hereby recognized as an area where the earth and its community of life are untrammeled by man, where man himself is a visitor who does not remain." By this definition, the Wilderness Covert is a wilderness, because man's works do not dominate the landscape, and nobody lives here. If the bridge is any indication, man's works are declining here—they're crumbling back into the earth.

We have, however, fashioned a more radical definition of wilderness since 1964. Ed Abbey argued that we needed areas of "absolute wilderness," where we didn't enter. He was fond of saying we should erect walls around our national parks and wilderness areas, and I agree we need areas we simply leave alone. Humans can utterly change the landscape, altering it in ways beyond that of floods, hurricanes, or wildfires. If nothing else, I believe, we need the idea of wilderness out there, even if we never go there, a thought many others have expressed.

What is here under my feet is not "absolute wilderness," but it does have a certain wildness. "We need the tonic of wildness," wrote Henry David Thoreau, "to wade sometimes in marshes where the bittern and meadow-hen lurk, and hear the booming of the snipe; to smell the whispering sedge where only some wilder and more solitary fowl builds her nest, and the mink crawls with its belly close to the ground."

I'm not out here wading marshes for bitterns and coots, but I do follow my dog through popple cuttings where ruffed grouse lurk or into the tag alders where woodcock probe for worms. This is my tonic, my antidote for too much time spent in a built landscape. Hunting, following the dog into this wildness, takes me to a place that's other than my own, and as such it is strange, mysterious, and sometimes frightening in its otherness. When I first step down a trail, there's an excitement about what I might discover, but also a slight dread of what to us is no longer familiar. It feels a bit like the start of a two-week vacation. It's our primordial fear of the un-known we never outgrow, and the more civilized we become the more unknowable—and fearful—places such as these become.

This place isn't without its dangers, hence the anxiety. A wolf pack roams this area, and earlier in the year this pack killed two bear hounds less than two miles from where we were walking, which is why I have Jenkins with me on this hunt. He works much closer to me than Fergus does. I think that in the rare event of a wolf attack, I could somehow defend him if I were close enough, which is probably feel-good nonsense. I could fall into the river and drown, contract Lyme disease from a tick bite, or be crushed by a falling tree. There are any number of ways to die or be injured out here, but the reality is we are much more likely to be plowed into by a texting teenager or drunken driver on the highway. This is Wisconsin, and we love our beer and our phones.

Thinking of beer, I realized I was laboring up the grade past the spot where the bird flushed behind me. I could see the boulders blocking the trail at the top of the hill. Up ahead, Jenkins turned back toward the trail, slowed, then stopped, front foot raised, his bell silent. His sides were heaving as he pulled in a scent so intoxicating it could stop him in his tracks. It was probably the old scent of the first bird we flushed a false point. After all, a dog's sense of smell is historical, which is why our dogs give us the once-over when we come home from work, the hospital, a bar. My dogs can detect where birds have been.

Several yards and several thoughts beyond Jenkins, a grouse roared up, surprising me, as is often the case. This time the bird did

Mark admires a mature ruffed grouse, a happy Jenkins sitting and waiting in the background. (Susan Parman)

not angle up the ridge sharply but veered a bit off the trail with little
or no cover between us. I tumbled the bird. Taking the bird from
Jenkins, I saw it was a gray beauty, a mature bird, with an unbroken
tail band. Holding it out, I let Jenkins bury his nose in the downy
breast feathers and suck in the intoxicating smell of grouse, of the
wildness neither of us wants to do without.

North

June Road

Ben and Jerry

Let's call them Ben and Jerry. Walking down June Road, I had just kicked a muddy and flattened ice cream container of Chubby Hubby, sending it spiraling into the ditch, and the name stuck. The two hunters and the ice cream brand were thereafter forever linked in my mind.

The irony was also appealing, because as I learned, these two were about the farthest a pair could get from the Vermont ice cream makers, and in more ways than geographically. Sure, northern Wisconsin is about as far as one can get from the East Coast, or the West Coast for that matter, but sometimes the Northwoods seems a different country entirely, speaking a different language and expressing a different culture, especially out in the backwoods. Which is most of northern Wisconsin.

Anyway, as their battered old 4 × 4 truck approached me upon our first meeting, I was trudging south down June Road, heading for home after a long and birdless hunt. They weren't approaching really, they were creeping along toward me, the truck groaning away in first gear. I called the dog over, latched onto his collar when he ran up to me, and waited on the shoulder of the road for the truck to pass so I could safely release the dog and continue on home. I had Ox that day, who sat, curiously watching the truck creeping north, and waited, showing much more patience than I.

This was over twenty years ago. Instantly, my hackles were up, along with my self-righteousness when it became obvious to me what they were doing. *Damn road hunters. Groundswatters.* As the old Chevy groaned toward me, I was planning my jeremiad, kicking over the blistering I would give these unsporting louts. *Where was the game warden when you really needed him*, I thought.

It must have been Jerry's smile, even though he was missing a couple of teeth, that immediately disarmed me, or possibly it was Maggie, Ben's black Lab circling around and squealing in the bed of the truck. She was wiggling around and banging her thick tail against the box as if she was keeping time to a song. "How's it going?" Jerry asked. I mumbled something incomprehensible under my breath, trying to make them realize I wanted to move on and have nothing to do with such scofflaws, but Jerry went on undeterred. "Nice looking dog? He point?" I still had Ox collared, and he was struggling to break my hold, clearly interested in Maggie.

They weren't breaking the law, since shooting a grouse on the ground is not illegal, nor was firing from the road we were on. Firing from a vehicle *is* illegal in Wisconsin, but I had not seen them do that. I took a lot of pride back then in my wing shooting and dog work—entirely too much, I now realize—and held all in contempt who did not hunt exactly as I did, all who did not keep the rules I deemed essential to grouse hunting. *I* gave the birds a sporting chance and *I* didn't murder them in cold blood pecking gravel in the ditch as these two did, cutting them down with nary a thought about fair chase.

Jerry, either not noticing my contempt or not caring about it, asked question after question about the dog, how we hunted, about my shotgun, what I did for a living, if I had children. By then, Ben, wearing an old army jacket with ANDERSON embroidered over the pocket, had shut off the engine and offered me a Bud Light (drinking and driving is also illegal in Wisconsin). They acted as if they had all day. I didn't ask them a single question, because I figured I knew all about their kind and how they hunted—the slow cruise down logging roads, beer between the legs, the shotgun slowly sliding out the window, and the dog leaping out of the box for the retrieve. They didn't even have to get out of the truck if they didn't care to. Maggie could do all the legwork. Oh, yes, I knew all there was to know about road hunting. And I thought I knew all there was to know about them and their kind.

A few years after this, I emerged from the brush along June Road—this time after a long but fruitful bushwhacking across a couple of steep ridges to the west of the road. I hit the road just in time to hear the brakes on Ben's truck howl to a stop. Only one of the brake lights was working. They had already gone past me and were a hundred yards to the north, so I started down the road toward home away from them, when they fired a shot. Gunnar, my Weimaraner, who was working the woods off the east side of the road and hadn't noticed the truck, leapt off the bank and onto the road, thinking it was me who had shot. He quickly realized we had company and tore up the road to investigate. *Oh great*, I thought. Maggie, in turn, had jumped out of the box and was searching the ditch for the bird. When Gunnar spotted her—or more likely smelled her—he beelined for her. He was a social dog. I had no choice but to turn back north and go after my dog.

When I got up to the truck, Maggie was back, bird in mouth, with Gunnar dancing around and sniffing her all over, more interested in dog than bird. I felt I had to be social, so I stepped up to the open window and said hello. "Any luck?" Jerry asked. It had been a good day, and I was all puffed up and feeling heroic—after all, I had three birds riding warmly against my back. I'm sure both Ben and Jerry noticed the bulge in my game bag. "You get yourself a new dog? I hope your old setter boy is all right?" As Jerry fired the questions at me, Maggie jumped up with her front paws on the passenger door and dropped the grouse through the open window and into Jerry's lap. "Good girl," he said, patting her on the head. Her muzzle had gone gray, but she still looked healthy and fit.

By the time we had parted, I had spread my three birds—two grays and one brown—across the warm hood of the Chevy, the engine ticking as it cooled, and Jerry was out of the cab limping around and admiring them, looking at their fans, pinching their bulging crops. He had even asked to see my Browning and swung it around at imaginary birds flushing along Jane Road. "Holy shit, this thing is lighter than a pool cue, lighter than my .45. No wonder you got all them partridge today. You should feel this thing, Ben." But Ben just sat in the driver's seat, took a slug of beer, and smiled, a worn 870 in the rack across the rear window. Maggie had trotted around to his side of the truck and jumped up on the driver's side door. Ben was stroking her head and murmuring something to her.

"You can have my birds if you want them," I said as we started to say our good-byes. They declined. "There's plenty of daylight left. We'll get a couple more no doubt before we call it quits," Jerry said. Sliding the birds back into my game bag, I realized how offensive my condescending offer had sounded. I walked away wondering if I had offended them, wondering why on earth I had showboated and displayed my birds on the hood of their truck.

In our last encounter, I almost didn't recognize Jerry since he was driving a different truck, an emerald green Ford F-150. It was, I could hardly believe, even more battered than the old Chevy. There was no dog in the open box, and no Ben. Jerry pulled up next to me and shut off the engine. "How's it going?" he asked. "Who's this?" he said, reaching out the window to Fergus, who was sniffing his outstretched hand. I told him about Fergus and Jenkins, our other setter. "Ferguson Jenkins," he cackled. "That's a good one. You think of that? Never took you for a Cubs fan. Me, I follow the Brewers." Jerry didn't ask about Ox and Gunnar.

"Where are your partners?" I asked.

Jerry hung his head and stared down at the floorboard of the truck. After a few seconds, the wind sighing through the white pine along the road, he fired up the truck, waved, and rolled on down

June Road. I haven't run into him since and never learned what happened to Ben and Maggie, so I had to make up the rest of the story based on that last look I had of Jerry's face as he drove off.

I figured Maggie was thirteen or fourteen by this time, which is about as long as we can hope a dog lives. Maybe she died one night peacefully in her sleep, and Ben found her when he woke the next morning. Even though Ben knew this was coming, he took it hard, like most hunters who love their dogs. She did his running around for him, fetching his birds because Ben had a nasty limp. I imagined he was shot in the hip in some long-forgotten conflict in the Middle East or with shrapnel from an RPG explosion.

Ben started to drink, even more than he already did to dull the pain in his leg, or perhaps he started in hard on the opiates. To this he added the pain in his heart for Maggie. Either way, one night a few weeks after Maggie's death, drunk or loaded on pills, he went swerving off the road and rammed his old Chevy head-on into an old, unforgiving white pine. That was the end of Ben and Jerry, and I wondered how long the Jerry half would survive. From the look of his face as he departed down June Road, not long.

In my mind, I wrote my name and phone number on a scrap piece of paper from my wallet and handed it to Jerry before he went silent and pulled away. "Give me a call sometime," I said. "My dogs don't retrieve worth a shit, but they sure do like to ride in the back of a truck, wind in their noses."

"I might do that," he said. I'm still waiting for Jerry to call.

The Triangle

Taking our trash to the Dumpster down on the corner—that's how we discovered woodcock singing in the Triangle. After supper on a warm April evening we decided to take a walk, and just before we left our cabin, I grabbed the garbage and said, "Let's kill two birds with one stone and walk by the Dumpster." We ending up killing three birds with one stone that evening.

There was a faint orange glow on the western horizon—Venus, Mars, and a few stars were visible overhead—as we came up to the Triangle after walking down our lane. It's about a quarter of a mile from our cabin down a narrow lane through deep forest, which then opens up as it runs by the Triangle. From there, we can see across the county highway to the neighbors' farm and the horses in their field.

Even before we got out of the woods and up to the clearing, we could hear the first *peent*, an unmistakable metallic sound. "You hear that?" I asked Susan. She hadn't. I stopped, set down the garbage, and motioned for Susan to stop. We stood in silence for several seconds— a light breeze from the southwest rattling the few dead oak leaves still clinging to the trees—until the next *peent*. "Woodcock," I mouthed to Susan, who can read lips from her years of experience on an oto-laryngology unit. She said something back to me, so I repeated, "Woodcock."

We quick-marched down to the Triangle to get closer. After a half dozen or so *peents*, the woodcock lifted out of the dead grass and withered flowers and spiraled up into the sky, his wings cheeping in the crepuscular light. He rose into the sky and fluted out his song above and dropped back to earth, fluttering down like a falling maple leaf. Transfixed, we watched the sky dance until the western horizon darkened inky black and signaled to the woodcock to end its mating flight for the day. I almost forgot to take the trash down to the Dumpster.

We don't hunt the Triangle. Come fall, no woodcock inhabit this place. We brought the dogs on leashes here once to witness the sky dance here, and they were a nuisance and a distraction. Now we leave them at home, which bothers them no end, and we can often hear them barking desperately in the background. Their lonesome barks carry well in the cool spring air. Our neighbors own the Triangle, a field maybe an acre large, bordered by gravel roads on two sides and brush and trees on its north side. It's a small slice of a once larger pasture, an old remnant of that field before the roads ran through it.

In summer, the Triangle is home to a riot of black-eyed Susans, bee balm, goldenrod, and asters swaying in warm breezes, but in April the field is dead, flat and matted, showing little if any green signs of life, other than the single immature white pine at the bottom of the triangle where the roads split. A few scattered bushes grow here and there, until the owners mow the field once again. In gray April, it's difficult to imagine late July. The woodcock's song and dance are the only flowering to make these gray days brighter.

Since the April evening twenty years ago when we discovered the woodcock singing, we came to the Triangle at least once each April to watch the show. That is, until the show abruptly ended a few years back. We had gotten used to watching the sky dance each spring and had begun to think it would always be so. But the cover surrounding the Triangle and the other adjacent fields had aged in those twenty years, and the surrounding woods had been little logged in that time. The adjacent aspen the woodcock used for feeding and cover had grown well past its prime as habitat, even though the Triangle had remained the same. Only the single white pine seemed to change—growing taller and spreading more like an oak than a white pine in the full sun. This aging of the aspen wood was inevitable, as it is in all of us, and even if the county logged some of it off, it would take a decade or more for it to hold woodcock reliably. By then, we would have other setters.

I was reaching for the handle of the front door to let the dogs inside. They had just finished their final pee and check on the neighborhood—our nightly ritual. It was mid-April, and here and there rotting snow still littered the woods, the remains of the deep drifts of a long winter winding down and losing its grip on the landscape. I had been collecting maple sap and boiling it down for several weeks.

As I turned the handle of the door, I heard it—a faint thread of flutelike notes high above the trees. It's unmistakable. I shoved the dogs inside and stepped back out on the stoop and waited. I was almost ready to go back in—it was getting cold standing there in just a long-sleeve T-shirt—when I heard the notes again overhead. I wasn't hearing things. This time there was no mistaking the woodcock. They were back. I ran inside, grabbed a coat, and yelled to Susan, "Woodcock!" I ran outside, jumped on my bike leaning against a tree, and pedaled down our gravel lane toward the Triangle. Susan followed as soon as she could find a coat and boots.

Down at the Triangle, we stood as still as possible next to the white pine, trying to blend in. I was holding my breath, peering west into the last of the evening light, my ears straining. And then we heard it, the *peent* on the ground coming from the middle of the Triangle. It's similar to the nighthawk's *peent* (described by Roger Tory Peterson) just before they swoop and dive on insects on warm and humid summer nights. Susan arrived out of breath, just as the male woodcock lifted off. There is no better description of this dance than Aldo Leopold's:

Suddenly the peenting ceases and the bird flutters skyward in a series of wide spirals, emitting a musical twitter. Up and up he goes, the spirals steeper and smaller, the twittering louder and louder, until the performer is only a speck in the sky. Then, without warning, he tumbles like a crippled plane, giving voice to a soft liquid warble that a March bluebird might envy. A few feet from the ground he levels off and returns to his peenting ground, usually to the exact spot where the performance began, and there he resumes his peenting.

When the woodcock lifted off, Susan and I moved out into the field, guessing where we thought the bird had been peenting. We stood exposed in the clearing, plainly in view of the woodcock, but our presence did not deter him, and he dropped back to this spot like a "crippled plane" tumbling to earth. We could hear the wind rushing through his wing feathers as he braked for his landing. We stood still as statues until the male resumed his peenting. This time we were so close I swear I could feel the metallic sound vibrate on my skin. He was so intent on finding a mate that he paid us no heed.

The woodcock lifted off again in a spiraling twitter and performed yet another sky dance for whatever female woodcock were watching on the sidelines of the Triangle. We gambled and moved even closer to the woodcock peenting ground. On his next fall, he dropped in over my shoulder less than two steps away. How could he be so little concerned about these lurking bipeds? Standing there, we tried not to wobble even as the wind in the open field buffeted us and knocked us off balance. Holding perfectly still with him peenting so close was like one of those moments in church when you try not to laugh and can't hold it back. When the bird lifted off once more, I told Susan we needed to step back a little. We were too close, and I didn't want the performance to end.

It went on for three more flights, until the light above the pines and spruce on the western horizon went from orange to deep blue, and the first few stars and planets were overhead. The eastern horizon back toward our cabin was full adult dark. Unable to see the road well enough to ride, we pushed our bikes home.

Without the woodcock, the Triangle was dead. The deafening silence there was once again full of the lusty song of emerging life. The sky dance reassured us that flowers would follow.

Yellow Gate

The Tragedy of Easy Access

When Gunnar spotted the mountain bikers at the top of the hill he tore off after them. I tried to collar him before he saw them, but I wasn't quick enough to grab him and he slipped away. Like a greyhound on the race track, he sprinted flat out toward them, the sand and small rocks thrown up from his paws showering me. He loved to run with me when I mountain biked, and he ran after any cyclist pedaling on the road past our house. Luckily, the mountain bikers were coming toward me rather than going away, else Gunnar might have disappeared over the hill with them.

I apologized profusely when they rolled up, but they seemed more amused than annoyed with Gunnar. They were bowhunting and using their mountain bikes to get deeper into the woods. I told them I occasionally used a mountain bike to bird hunt since Gunnar loved to do both things. As they were leaving, one of them said, "You know, it would be a whole lot easier if they just opened the gate. It used to be open all of the time. We could just drive right up here then." I laughed and said, "Sure, but then there'd be a whole lot more people back in here." He nodded, and they pedaled away.

Yellow Gate is sizable chunk of public land of around twenty thousand acres encompassing a four-thousand-acre lake. The Wisconsin DNR manages both the water and the land, and I think they do a good job at this sometimes thankless task. It's impossible to please all of the Yellow Gate user groups; someone will always have a gripe. For instance, ATVers would love to have access to the entire twenty thousand acres, but the DNR restricts their access to the eastern side of the property—part of the reason the property is gated (at times). Unlike the overseers of county and sometimes national forests, the DNR is serious about keeping motorized traffic out of nonmotorized areas. Their gates are stout and strategically placed, nearly impossible for a vehicle to drive around. I know of only one county that enforces its nonmotorized areas like the DNR. Most counties are much more lax, or don't have the resources to enforce their bans when it comes to policing nonmotorized areas.

The locked gate frankly pisses off a lot of people. It's about five miles from the gate and the parking area on the eastern side to the western boundary. This upsets many deer hunters and even some up-land hunters. We all want easy access, at least for ourselves. The first time I encountered the open gate, I, too, drove deep into the cover to hunt—as did several other groups of hunters that Saturday. That was the busiest time I had ever experienced at Yellow Gate, shotguns going off every few moments like it was the opening day of pheasant season in Iowa. I didn't return for several seasons after this, until I heard the gate was once again closed and locked.

The first time I hunted Yellow Gate over twenty years ago, I wasn't initially impressed with the bird numbers there. For the most part, it's one huge aspen cutting, a vast monoculture of evenly aged trees. There are isolated pockets of older hardwoods that haven't seen a chainsaw in years and, therefore, are not worth hunting, except maybe along their edges where they butt up against the popple. A maze of trails and logging roads spur off Yellow Gate Road and wind through the aspen, and if there were more mixed cover, this place would be crawling with ruffed grouse. The occasional red pine, balsam fir, or red oak mixes in with the aspen, but not enough of these other species have established themselves to attract high numbers of ruffed grouse. I always expect to see many more than we do.

The woodcock numbers at Yellow Gate, however, have impressed me a few times. Twice, I've had days of over fifty points. After these hunts, I starting calling this place the Yellow Brick Road. I can honestly say there can be too much of a good thing when it comes to woodcock, especially as a young man with a strong ruffed grouse bias. Back then, I thought that after shooting my limit of woodcock, all of those woodcock points were simply distractions for the real main course—ruffed grouse. Yet in time, I came to value Yellow Gate for what it was, a woodcock haven. I would take family and friends who wanted to get in some shooting there, or a young dog needing some consistent work and bird contact. It was a great place to train a pup.

On one hunt at Yellow Gate we let three-month-old Jenkins trail Fergus around in three inches of early October snow as the older, veteran dog pointed woodcock after woodcock hunkering in the snow. We whoa-ed Jenkins behind each Fergus point, flushed the bird, and watched Jenkins tear off after the woodcock on his short legs. He didn't point a bird that day, but we knew he had a keen prey drive. We played that game until we were wet to the knees and cold. The dogs would have kept going.

Without the gate and restricted access, I wonder if the woodcock would have been as thick as they were. Word about hot spots tends to get out among bird hunters, and with unlimited access, it would be possible to shoot out a local population. This situation reminds me of the tragedy of the commons, an economic theory ecologist Garrett Hardin made popular in the late 1960s. Titled after an 1833 pamphlet written by the English economist William Forster Lloyd, the theory claims individual users will exploit a shared resource for their own good even to the point of spoiling that resource for others. Our collective actions destroy the birds we love, something we would not do as individuals.

It's unlikely an individual hunter could damage a local woodcock or grouse population over the course of the season, although this is possible in smaller coverts. It's more likely collective pressure would destroy it. We know how many birds we are shooting, but we don't know the cumulative impact of other hunters. We can limit our take, but not theirs. Plus, sometimes when we know other hunters are having success in a given place, we rush there to get a slice of the pie before it's all gone, escalating the pressure on the birds. Such is the dilemma of public lands with open and easy access.

It's much easier to manage wildlife on private land closed to all except the owner(s), but, of course, many of us cannot afford to own private land, and few of us own the vast acreage necessary to grouse and woodcock hunt. It makes sense for a deer hunter to own forty or eighty acres because in Wisconsin this much land can supply a deer or two each year without hurting the long-term population. Upland hunters require much larger tracts of land. Throughout the grouse and woodcock season, I roam thousands of acres seeking these birds, walking probably well over one hundred miles per season (I should measure it some year) in pursuit of a few dozen birds.

Because we are all pursuing a limited resource, the DNR gates this public land and restricts access, in order to avoid the tragedy of wiping out the local grouse and woodcock populations. And I'm OK with this—for now. As I age and my hips and knees go bad, I might change my mind and join the chorus who regularly castigates the DNR. Then, increased access might seem a fair trade for more traffic and crowds of hunters.

Last year, we returned to Yellow Gate after several years' absence. It was a hot and humid day in late September. We were on our way to our cabin and decided to stop off and hunt in the relative cool of the early morning. By the time we made the trek all the way to our cabin, it would have been too hot to hunt, at least for Fergus. Then again, I'm not at all fond of upland hunting when the temperature rises above sixty.

The gate was open when we pulled up to it—an ominous sign. We had heard the DNR had once again closed the gates to restrict access, which was why we stopped by, but this was obviously not true. We decided to hunt anyway; we were here. So we drove down the road a mile or so past the open gate, parked, and set off with both Fergus and Jenkins.

In an hour and a half, we put up a handful of woodcock and shot a pair. We didn't flush a single grouse. Even with a heavy dew that soaked the dogs' coats as well as our brush pants, Fergus was struggling with the heat by ten o'clock, so we decided to pack up and head north to our cabin and hope for a cool evening. Maybe we could get out with Jenkins, who does better in the heat than Fergus.

Driving out, we agreed the woodcock numbers were down compared with the best years at Yellow Gate, those miraculous fifty-point days. Several factors could have been responsible: aging cover, disease, predation—both animal and human—plus the woodcock had yet to start their migration and we were hunting the smaller local population. Or maybe we were just hunting in the wrong place at the wrong time. Still, I blamed the open gate and the easy access. You could drive right up to the best cover. In the good old days of high bird numbers, we would get woodcock points five yards off Yellow Gate Road.

"I wish the clowns at the DNR would lock the gate and throw away the key," I said, going off about how too many hunters were getting in here and how they had shot out all the birds. They were ruining things. Never mind that I was guilty of doing the same. The old story of the tragedy of the commons, or at the very least the tragedy of easy access, was playing out—or so I thought.

Susan said I sounded like one of the barstool fools holding forth at amateur hour at a local bar. I had arrived at old coot status. "Besides," she said, "when you're an old man, then you'll whine about the gate being locked." I said nothing and pointed the truck north. What could I say? She was right.

SOUTH

Badwater Creek

Against Grouse Hunting

Ah, the noble sport, the noble bird. Paeans have been written to the king of game birds, the ruffed grouse, recollected in the tranquility of air-conditioning, central heat, or maybe before a crackling fire and with a tumbler of bourbon. It's mostly horseshit penned by pink-palmed romantics for like-minded suckers. Years of grouse hunting in northern Wisconsin have taught me one thing—it's a lot of walking over rough country, punctuated by the occasional shot, followed by the inevitable cursing. My years afield chasing the noble bird have turned me into a hard-boiled realist, despite my soft spot for English setters.

Take this late September hunt, for example. Wet from the chest down, I popped out on the gravel road and started clomping back toward my truck, a white speck on the horizon. I had had enough fun for one day. With every heavy step, water squished between my toes in my sodden wool socks, and my wet hunting pants clung to my thighs, chafing my sweet meat, that tender baby skin area inside and above the knees.

The dense air felt more like dull July than sharp and crisp autumn. This morning a heavy dew dripped off every leaf and every branch of every popple and showered me as I banged my way through the skinny trees to reach each of Fergus's points. It would be dry in the woods by early afternoon, and I thought about waiting until then to hunt, but by noon the temperature would rise into the low seventies, and the woods would feel like a sauna. Pick your poison—wet and warm or hot and dry. Fergus, my big, heat-intolerant English setter, could only handle the relative cool of this September morning.

Fergus, eternally optimistic and a romantic at heart, continued to work the brush, paralleling me as I made my way down the road toward my truck. At least the walking was easier out on the road rather than down there in the tangle where the dog was thrashing around. It was surprising Fergus didn't injure himself, the way he attacked an aspen cutting.

Our last point had been particularly aggravating. His bell had stopped ringing, and I stood there on the road a few moments to make sure he wasn't moving. "Fergus?" I called out a couple of times. To be certain he wasn't faking, I waited some more. A plane droned overhead and fouled up my hearing. I was sure Fergus was on another damn woodcock, whose season didn't begin until next week. He had pointed a good dozen this morning, each and every one a distraction from the real game—ruffed grouse. I thought I had picked a covert where we wouldn't encounter the little bog suckers, but here they lived aplenty, driven here to higher ground by recent heavy rains, what felt like Bengali monsoons.

I decided to wait him out this time. The last thing I wanted to do was work down to Fergus through all the heavy cover just to kick up another twittering woodcock. True, he looks like a magazine cover locked up in a classic point, but you see one point, you've seen them all. Surely, I was jaded.

In addition, Fergus was on the far side of the creek meandering through the cover, a creek I would have to ford or leap across to get to the dog, and then there was all that popple to try and slip through without getting yet another stream of water down my back. *Come on, Fergus, bust that bird. Come on.* I stood on that gravel road at least two minutes, hoping the dog would break point, but Fergus held fast and did his job. There was no other course but to get to the dog, drunk on woodcock scent.

The creek was running high from all the recent rain and too deep to ford, so I had to pick my line across the moss-covered rocks before leaping. But that mattered little as I slipped off a rock in the middle of the stream and plunged into the creek—appropriately named the Badwater—and swamped my rubber boots, which wasn't all that disastrous since my feet were already soaked from the water wicked by my pants and socks down into my boots and pooling around my toes. What was a little more water?

Out of the creek on the other bank and up into the popple, I finally spotted Fergus through the trees. Okay, maybe I'm not so jaded after all, as I did get some consolation and enjoyment standing there and observing the intensity of his point, which he had held for several minutes, not unusual for the close-sitting woodcock. I, gun on my shoulder, took in this tableau so at the very least I could return home with this mental picture. I couldn't eat it, but it was something. His head was lower than his flat-out tail, slight curl at the tip, and his left hind leg was lifted, hanging there as if stepping down would be upon hot coals. I wondered how long he could hold such a pose before getting a cramp in that leg.

At that moment, a grouse burst up in the interval between us, cleared the aspens into the haze of the September sky, and disappeared. Just like that, it was gone, as if it had been raptured into heaven. All was silent, except the rattling of the aspen leaves, the quaking aspen mocking me. I didn't even get my gun off my shoulder. Instead of praising the dog for holding a point on a grouse for several minutes, I cursed and wailed and scanned the cutting for a tree large enough to bash my shotgun against. Lucky for me, none of the aspen whips were larger around than a broomstick or my Browning might have been history. I called the dog over, put him on heel, and made straight out of the woods for the road.

I was almost to the truck when I heard a vehicle coming from the west, so I called to Fergus and collared him. The vehicle stopped alongside me and the driver rolled down the passenger-side window. "Pretty wet, ain't it?" he said, looking at my pants. I could see a scoped rifle lying across the console. *No shit*, I thought. "Hey, I don't mean to scare you out of here, but I had nine wolves on my trail cam over my bait pile last night. It's about a mile straight north of here." I had worked at least halfway that direction earlier in our hunt. Images of Fergus set upon by a large pack of ravenous wolves scrolled across my mind. They could hamstring him and rip him to pieces in seconds. I shuddered at the thought.

"Thanks for the info," I said.

"My buddy had fifteen in his alfalfa field a couple of nights ago," he said. "His farm is north of the highway, maybe three miles from here. I ain't trying to scare you outta here, but I thought you should know."

"Well, shit," I said, this time out loud, as he rolled up his window, waved, and drove on.

With Fergus safe in the back of the truck, I checked him over before shutting the topper door. He had cut his foot, but at least there were no ticks crawling all over his coat. At least for now, anyway. The bloodsucking hordes would amass later in October.

Much has been written in praise of grouse hunting, more so than any other kind of upland hunting. My shelves are full of books on this most principled of blood sports—William Harnden Foster, Burton Spiller, George Bird Evans, Charles Norris, Corey Ford, Gene Hill, William Tapply, and Frank Woolner. And those are just the old dead guys. I myself am guilty of contributing to this ever-expanding tradition, this accumulation of words and stories and romantic notions. Despite the dozens of books and millions of words, I don't know if I have ever read anything *against* grouse hunting.

The ruffed grouse is one of the most difficult upland birds to consistently bring to hand, proving, I suppose, that absence makes the heart grow fonder. William Harnden Foster writes that the grouse hunter "walks miles and miles toward the unexpected burst of the great bird that he dreams about in his sleep, ignobly misses it as it rips through the cover, and is left standing in his tracks, shaking and half-blind with excitement. He calls the grouse a hard mark, and so it may be always." Foster neglected to mention all the tired, aching muscles and the worn-out boots.

George Bird Evans writes, "There is nothing sensible about grouse hunting and a man can't be entirely sane who will put himself through what he calls the pleasures of sport. . . . One season I hunted grouse in deep snow for twenty-eight days and fired exactly three shells. Only the dedicated are grouse hunters." Foster's and Evans's quotes sum up the average grouse hunter's experience—the miles and miles of walking, over rough country in all kinds of weather, only to have the one bird you see all day leave you feeling as if you had just been struck by lightning. Even if you do get a shot off, it's at a bird flushing, flaring, and darting through a temperate-zone rain forest. You count yourself lucky to scratch down a few feathers.

This happened to me just recently. Fergus pointed a bird, and I shot it as it rose above the aspens, clearly rocking the bird and cutting a few feathers, but the bird flew on. We followed the bird up, and soon Fergus pointed again. I moved up past the pointing dog and walked a wide circle around the dog. When I got back to the dog, I noticed one single gray tail feather a couple of steps in front of the dog. I picked the feather up and brought it home, my trophy for the day. Miles of walking and one tail feather. I stuck it between the panes of the kitchen window as a reminder—it's still there—but its wisdom hasn't kept me out of the woods.

Unlike the good old days of grouse hunting, these days, at least in the Upper Midwest, we have to contend with timber wolves, ticks, and the West Nile virus. The old dead guys never wrote about these threats, since the worst they had to contend with were pesky mosquitoes and the rare coyote. Instead, they wrote about the blazing autumnal colors, abandoned apple orchards, stone fences, and rare

English side-by-side shotgun. And we sucked it all in, around a humming woodstove in January and in a porch rocker in July. But this all begs the question, have we been duped?

With Fergus in the back of the truck, I decided to drive down along the river and up around to the north toward the area where the bear hunter said he had captured the wolves on his trail cam. Halfway north along the river, a grouse darted out of the tag alders, bored across the road, and missed the windshield by a beak's length. Its gray tail flared as it banked to escape the oncoming two tons of metal, barely clearing the corner of the hood. I skidded to a stop on the gravel, jammed the truck in reverse, and backed up. I looked left into the brush where the big gray bird had flown, then into the right ditch. Nothing. But just before I put the truck in gear and rolled on down the road, I noticed movement in the passenger-door mirror— it was the trailing bird, clucking around in the ditch, unsure of its next move.

Backing up, I rolled down the passenger window and came up even with the grouse. It stood there, cocking its hatchet head to the right and the left. My shotgun and shells were lying just behind my seat in the extended cab. I wondered if I could ease the gun out of the case and load it without spooking the bird. I looked up and down the road—no cars in sight—and thought how easy it would be to slide the gun out the window and execute the bird with a single shot. A woof from Fergus in the back of the truck flushed the bird and made the decision for me.

Driving home, I replayed in my mind the film of the suicidal grouse streaking across the road. I could see the individual tail feathers bending and separating as the bird ruddered itself out of harm's way. It banked away from my truck, then up and over the tag alders in the ditch, before dropping back down into the cover. It was the best look at a ruffed grouse I had had all season. We had put up plenty of grouse, both Fergus and Jenkins pointing their fair share of birds. I had nearly stepped on several before they flushed, and I had yet to catch even a silhouette in the thick cover. I was hearing a lot of birds yet seeing none clearly. So far that season, I had fired once at a fleeting shape crossing twenty-five yards away from me. This was as close as we had come to bagging a bird. It wasn't twenty-eight days and only three shots, but there was a lot of the season left to yet match Evans's mark.

Was I a fool to walk up birds with a pointing dog? Why not cruise northern Wisconsin backroads and roll up unawares on ditch birds clucking alongside the road? This, too, is a time-honored grouse-hunting tradition in the state. We have been employing this mode of hunting even before cars and trucks were commonplace, using the horse and buggy instead of the internal combustion motor. I once heard an old man tell of how his family used to drive their buggy eight miles into Mellen, Wisconsin, and pot grouse the entire way, shooting whatever guns they had, but a .22 was best. Ammunition was cheap and it provided a clean head shot that didn't waste any of the precious breast meat. When they got to town, they sold the birds and bought supplies.

Another friend was eating a hamburger and fries in a bar in Park Falls when a guy riding an ATV banged in the door for a beer—well, maybe more than one. He spoke in a loud bar voice, making sure everyone in the joint knew that just as soon as he knocked back a few tappers he was going out to get his hundredth partridge. "Boy, them timber chickens sure is stupid," he said. Truth be told, the king of the gamebirds does lapse into stupidity around vehicles, sensing no danger from the occupants within bent on murder. It's so easy to idle along logging roads and trails, shotgun ready to go, and groundswat unwary birds, especially since it is now legal in Wisconsin to have an uncased firearm in a vehicle. They say a sawed-off 28 gauge or .410 is best, but the ammo sure is expensive for such tiny shells. With a century of this hunting technique on our backroads, it seems evolution should have wiped out all of these stupid genes in grouse, but each year there seems to be a steady crop of dim-witted birds pecking gravel along our roads. Survival of the fittest doesn't seem to apply in this case.

I wasn't against grouse hunting—the passion for it still flamed in my chest—but I was tempted to change my tactics because so far that season, my tactics weren't working, and moreover, I wasn't having any fun doing what I was doing. And I bet that guy on the ATV had racked up a couple of dozen kills already this early in the season. Why beat my head against a rock or, more to the point, flail myself in the popple thickets or bloody myself in blackberry canes? Why march for miles in rough country for one or two shots at a bird I might only hear? Why put my dogs in harm's way, exposing them to ticks and wolves? Or for that matter, why expose myself to the same risks? I could simply load the dogs up in the back of the truck, fill the tank, spread a handful of shells on the passenger seat, and cruise the backroads looking for mentally challenged grouse. Once in a while, the dogs could jump out for a retrieve, possibly even work a ditch or two if I thought it worthwhile. You can't say such a method doesn't have appeal.

The next day I had to work, but the following morning, I woke up to a beautiful fall day. The skies had cleared overnight, and a light frost coated the grass. That was the end of our tomatoes, beans, and cucumbers, but it seemed a fair trade. A cool north wind was blowing down from Canada, and setter-tail clouds drifted across the blue above, surely a sign for a grouse-hunting fool such as me. Against grouse hunting? Not today, not me.

Elbow Creek

Windfall

My setter was maybe fifty feet from me on the edge of the cover between the creek and the clear-cut—he was pointing, tail curved slightly above horizontal. From my vantage point on top of the low-slung bank, I could just make out through the brush his white form below, but getting to him would be another matter. It took me at least a minute to reach the dog, shinnying up on top of the larger recumbent logs and dropping over their bulk. I also had to slither under the trees still hung up in others, their limbs tangled, true widow makers. Scooting underneath one such maple tree, I snagged my game bag on a branch and had to lay down my shotgun and twist into a yoga position, using both hands to extricate myself. *I'm coming, Fergus. Hang on just a little longer.*

Fergus did hold on, and as I hopped down off a log next to him, the brush rattled, and, as if on cue, out flushed the first ruffed grouse of the day. I didn't even see the bird until it was out of range and flying right-to-left across the creek, not that I was in any position to shoot. Fergus took a few steps in the direction of the flushing bird as two more birds broke right, away from the creek toward the clear-cut in the opposite direction of the first bird. I pivoted, locked in a dance with the closest bird, tracking it through the brush. However, the bird never flew out into the open of clear-cut where I was expecting to get a shot at it. *Where did it go?*

Moving in the bird's direction, I started to wonder if I was seeing things, or maybe the bird was beamed into some other reality. After working over toward where I last saw the bird, I spotted the grouse perched in a tree at the edge of the clear-cut, cocking its head around nervously. The bird had braked suddenly and landed in a tree, smart enough not to risk the exposure of the fresh clear-cut. Fergus closed in on the tree where the jumpy grouse had perched, oblivious to its presence, moving until I whoa-ed him. I took a few more steps toward the bird, then stopped and flicked off the safety on my Browning. A few more tense steps and abruptly the grouse flushed and broke across the opening, straining with all its life toward the cover a hundred yards away.

It never made it that far, as I tumbled the bird maybe twenty yards from the perching tree and dropped it in the tangle of the fresh clear-cut. The shot echoed across the creek bottom and a few feathers twirled down in the clear November air as Fergus rushed over to search the clotted logging slash. As far as shots at ruffed grouse go, they don't get any more wide open, any "easier," and I was surprised I didn't blow it. Some grouse hunters pass up shots on a treed bird, shooting only birds pointed or flushed by their dogs fair and square, but I had clawed through the clear-cut for that bird and had bloody scratches on hands and face to prove as much, and Fergus had pointed it originally. My rules were subjective and arcane—even mysterious to me at times—but, after flushing this ruffed grouse, I wasn't about to let it get away without a shot.

For the twenty years I've hunted here, Elbow Creek has always been rough cover and difficult to hunt—tag alders and hazelnut down along the creek with aspen, balsam fir, blackberry canes, and other assorted brush mixed in with mature timber on the higher banks— but when straight-line winds ripped through the area a few summers back, it turned the entire covert into a twisted and tangled nightmare. The latest windfall has made parts of it nearly impenetrable, but I know I can always count on it for birds, and so I come here like an addict looking for a fix.

The county logged most of the land after the blowdown, all except a narrow strip along the creek where they must have thought it too steep or too wet to log. Or perhaps the land managers wanted a buffer along the creek. The windfall of maple, cherry, hemlock, and yellow birch—some of the downed trees thirty inches in diameter—was a boon to a local sawmill and area woodworkers, and the clear-cut will make this cover even more productive in the years to come, a blessing to upland hunters. Even though walking through a fresh clear-cut through all of the slash is difficult, it's relatively easy compared with navigating the tangle of the creek bottom. The birds love that blowdown cover, more like a fortress than a covert.

The new growth in the clear-cut isn't much more than knee high, like a cornfield in July, and the aspen shoots offer about as much protection. But in just a few years things will change—these shoots will be head high and in a few more years as high as a basketball hoop. The thick shoots will make moving through there a chore, but even more birds will move in, both woodcock and grouse. The edge cover between the uncut blowdown along the creek and the aspen clear-cut—that's the line I will take through here. By then, Fergus and Jenkins will be gone, and I will most likely ramble through it with another setter not yet born.

On a Sunday afternoon in early June 2016, after a late lunch, I lay down for a nap with Fergus and Jenkins on the bed in the spare bedroom. We had been lying there only a few moments when the sky darkened and the wind started to rise. Then the rain started to tinkle on the metal roof. No storm warnings were posted, and it had been a mostly sunny day until then. As the gusts increased in strength, I sat up and looked out the north window, peering into the gale-driven rain. Our backyard was a churning of green trees. An enormous CRACK followed the next nasty gust, and the tree I just happened to be looking at out the north window snapped in two like the proverbial toothpick and toppled to the east with a boom, wedging itself between two larger oaks. (This maple was twenty-seven inches in diameter breast high.)

I jumped off the bed and yelled, "*Run!*" Stepping on my heels, the dogs fled down the hall with me toward the basement. They sensed excitement or fear in my voice. Jenkins, as he danced down the hall by my side, looked up at me, wondering what the commotion was all about, instantly ready for it. Susan, who had lain down in our upstairs bedroom, came leaping two-by-two down the stairs. Running down the hall, I saw out of the corner of my eye through the living-room picture window half a tree fall in the front yard and heard and felt the shock of it hitting the house. The floor shuddered. By the time we got down into the basement, the storm had passed, gone as quickly as it had blown up, and in five minutes we were out in the yard surveying the damage.

At first sight, it was inconceivable, overwhelming. It made me want to sit down and weep. We lost six mature trees—and countless smaller ones—the largest a red oak over thirty-six inches in diameter, a tree I dubbed Moby Dick, a whale of a tree that knocked down the majority of the trees we lost, the smaller ones like bowling pins or dominos. The downed trees covered our entire backyard, obliterating our garden and raspberry patch. Inexplicably, the trees missed the chain-link fence of our old dog kennel, no consolation since the dogs live in the house with us. The straight-line winds did spare the smaller maples (my sugar trees) east of the driveway, but they had savaged our biggest maple just east of the house, the ancient tree throwing the massive limb that struck the house and ruined the roof. Most of it is still standing, but it will have to go now that it is damaged. I hate to cut it since it shades the house and is my best sugar tree, but it's clearly a danger to us and the house. We now have a hole in the sky in our backyard, and I miss those massive oaks, but they didn't fall for naught.

A windfall can be defined as a dividend, a bonanza, or sometimes as a piece of luck or manna from heaven. So far, I have twenty saw logs, which I plan to mill up into lumber. I also have several years' worth of firewood, probably four or five full cords, so we won't be cold for some time. The dogs will warm their bones in the radiating heat of our Norwegian woodstove on cold winter mornings for several years to come, and I will remember the big oaks that stood here for over one hundred years. After counting the rings of Moby Dick, I understood it was a sapling around the time of the Civil War. To the east, I could look out over the valley of the Wisconsin River and wonder what had stood here at that time.

According to *An Exaltation of Larks*, the collective noun for woodcock is "fall, " as in a fall of woodcock, which brings to mind more than anything a soft overnight fall of snow that gracefully blankets the earth. Flight birds truly are a windfall. A few times in my life, fewer than I can count on one hand, I have wandered into areas thick with grouse, coveys of grouse (a "drumming, " according to *An Exaltation of Larks*), but these have been nothing like the falls of woodcock I've come across through my years of hunting. Woodcock can materialize suddenly, then disappear just as suddenly, here today gone tomorrow, like a spring snow. When they do appear in flights, their numbers can be truly staggering.

Woodcock, in these times of overwhelming abundance, seem like manna from heaven, a gift from above. It surprised me to learn that quail are also part of the manna story in Exodus. Not only did the Lord promise the Israelites manna from heaven when the dew of the morning had dried, but also quail in the evening so they could eat meat. "At twilight you shall eat flesh, and in the morning you shall be filled with bread" (Exodus 16:12). According to the Old Testament story, Israel would have quail for supper and manna, a white flaky honey bread spiced with coriander, for breakfast, perhaps the harbinger of our habit of breakfast cereal in the morning and chicken or hamburgers in the evening.

But many years later, Israel tired of the manna from heaven and complained to the Lord: "But now our strength is dried up, and there is nothing at all but this manna to look at" (Numbers 11:6). The Israelites fondly recalled the fish, the cucumbers, the leeks, onions, and garlic they used to eat back in Egypt. Actually the author of Numbers writes that the "rabble . . . had a strong craving, and the people of Israel also wept again and said, 'Oh that we had meat to eat!'" (Numbers 11:4). The twilight quail had disappeared, and Israel was forced to go on a vegetarian diet. The rabble was roused, and I can't blame them. After all, they had been promised by the Lord a nightly windfall of quail. I can appreciate their disappointment—I know what it feels like to hunt a promising covert and not put up a single grouse.

When the storm passed and we surveyed the damage in our backyard, we were initially stunned, then devastated. We were more concerned about the damage to our trees than that to our house. It would take a month or so to fix the house; it took over a century to grow many of the fallen trees. We loved those old trees, and there they were laid down, tossed around like matchsticks, ruined. We also lost our herb garden and our raspberries, which in a good year would produce between eight and ten gallons of fruit. At first, I didn't even know where to start cutting in order to begin the lengthy cleanup. We revere big, mature trees, and centuries ago a few cults worshipped them. The blowdown in our backyard showed me how much I cared about my old trees, but it also taught me the value of the windfall and the new growth that follows.

We plan to use the red oak lumber we mill up for an addition to our cabin, what a friend calls our grouse camp. We filled our woodshed with the sweet-smelling oak and staked out a half-dozen face cords beside the shed, and still we had beaver stacks of split wood lying next to the downed trees. It was a bonanza of firewood, and there's much comfort in seeing all that stacked and dry wood—it's better than money in the bank.

Three months later there's already new growth sprouting where the old trees stood, new habitat for backyard fauna. The raspberries came back almost immediately, and maple and ash whips seemed to sprout overnight. We were even able to salvage some parsley, thyme, oregano, and cilantro from our herb garden crushed under the fallen oaks.

Not that long ago, before chainsaws, high winds and fire made the clearings necessary for the wildlife that depend on young growth— like grouse and woodcock. A windfall of trees, in turn, yields a windfall of birds. I love the smell and look of northern red oak. It heats our home like no other firewood, and yet there's beauty and majesty in an ancient oak standing, which is why we love to walk beneath great trees and look up into their arms.

On the other hand, there's a different kind of beauty in a blowdown or a clear-cut—in the new life that follows in the wake of falling trees. This should be obvious to a grouse and woodcock hunter like me, but sometimes it's difficult to see the life of the forest through all the trees—especially when they're old friends lying on the ground, lifeless and still.

Homestretch Patch

The Homestretch Patch is just that—a trifling two-acre patch of recently logged brush. It's bordered north and south by two cross-country ski trails and surrounded by mature maple and popple woods. This patch in the county forest lies about a half mile from the finish line of a loop used for many types of silent sport races—cross-country running and skiing, plus mountain biking. People walk their dogs and hike here, they pick raspberries in the thickets, and gun deer hunters swarm the place for a week in mid-November. This covert, close to the trailhead and the warming hut there, sees heavy multiple use in all seasons, so with all the surrounding human activity, it's unlikely grouse cover.

Which is why I was so surprised to put up a ruffed grouse here in such a well-trafficked area. I was humping it by the patch, intent on getting to what I considered "real" grouse cover a couple of miles deeper into the forest, away from the well-worn paths and playgrounds close to the warming hut and parking lots. It was Fergus, however, who pulled me into the patch, following a scent trail into the brush. I would have hustled right by, but he flashed a couple of points right off the trail and moved deeper into the hazelnut and popple, clearly on the scent of something he thought important. I wasn't thrilled about his detour but followed him anyway. You would think after all the years of hunting behind him, I would trust him more. After all, he is the one with the shrewd and discriminating nose.

Once before cleaning the birds, I stuck my nose into a grouse's feathers and then a woodcock's to see if I could tell the difference. The grouse smelled like a musty bedspread, and the woodcock made me sneeze. But Fergus's sense of smell is multilayered and multidimensional. I imagine he could smell the difference between brown-phased and gray-phased ruffed grouse, as we can taste the difference between a pilsner and a stout. He could smell the mud on a woodcock's toes and know that three hours earlier it had been dining on worms beneath tag alders. He could probably smell the type of worm on its breath.

Nose pulling him along, Fergus got ahead of me and out of sight. Then his bell went silent, and a half minute later I found him locked up, his flews and sides heaving, head low. This looked serious. I worked a semicircle around his front side and came back up facing him, my thumb on the top tang of the action of my Browning, ready in an eye blink to flick off the safety. Nothing happened. As I stood there and looked at the surrounding brush, wondering if we had a false point, Fergus, still rigid, turned his head slightly to the left and down. His nose was pointing at a downed oak branch, the withered leaves still on, about five yards away off his right shoulder. *No, it couldn't be there*, I thought as I slipped around him and took a step toward the branch. The ground exploded in front of me, and the bird was in the air. Collecting myself, I swung on the bird and dumped it with the first barrel. Fergus raced over and stood over the brown bird, nosing it as it beat its wings in the spent oak and aspen leaves.

Picking up the now still bird and admiring its fan and mottled breast feathers—the very colors of autumn—the words of Aldo Leopold came to mind: "Yet subtract the grouse and the whole thing is dead. An enormous amount of some kind of motive power has been lost." I had subtracted a grouse and, holding the lifeless bird, part of me wished I hadn't. Sure, I was elated to bring that grouse to hand, and I love to eat them, but if it had been possible, I would have made the bird whole again and released it into the autumn sky. This is not how our world is made, however. I could no sooner restore it to life than restore a falling star in the night sky. The grouse in my hand had flown its last flight, its wings beating its death throes in the leaf litter, trying to escape one more time to freedom.

I'm not squeamish about killing birds. It was more about the place where I had killed this grouse. It was almost as if I had killed a neighbor, a friend. I would ski, run, or ride by this spot many times in years to come, and I preferred to think of this place as home to a resident ruffed grouse, not as a place that once had a bird living there. Subtract the bird and the "whole thing was dead." I wanted to see its tracks across the blue-tinged snow of January or hear it drumming at trillium time in May, but you can't have your grouse and kill it too.

After pocketing the bird, we set off deeper into the woods, toward the cover where we had originally planned to hunt. First, we went down along a creek bordered by balsam fir and tag alders with popple up on the higher and drier land of the banks. Typically when we moved birds here, they flew off to the north into private land, but I always return, hoping for that one chance, for a bird that would peel off back over onto public land.

After striking out here, we worked a low hill into prime cover deeper into public land. Over the years, I had shot over a dozen birds in this reliable friend. It was never a honey hole, and usually a place I visited late in the season, but it was always worth a flush or two and often it told a good story. Once I shot a woodcock here, saw it tumble, and inexplicably couldn't find it. We looked a half hour for that bird until I finally looked up and spotted it dangling from a limb, caught by a leg as it fell in death.

We worked around the hill with no result and then down along another smaller creek that fed into the larger one we had worked previously. We were almost back to the larger creek when Fergus started to creep around and make game. I had hunted around him for so long—eight seasons—I knew he was on hot scent. Shortly, he

A shot woodcock dangles from an aspen, caught by a leg as it fell. (Mark Parman)

was on point, nose lifted into a slight breeze. I worked a ten-yard circle around the dog through thick popple, gun at port arms, thumb on the safety. This was what we had come for. This took a minute or so as I had to shoulder my way through the broomsticks and pick up my hat when it was ripped off my head, sure the birds would flush at that moment, as I reached down and snatched it up by the brim — one eye on the hat, the other scanning the immediate, ready for the flush.

By the time I had circled back around to Fergus, just as earlier, the tension had drained out of my arms. Just as I was about to tap him on the head and tell him to hunt on, a bird jumped out of a small patch of marsh grass five yards behind the dog. The bird banged low through the popple for twenty yards or so, then popped out above the trees on the edge of the range of my cylinder-choked 20 gauge, but I threw a Hail Mary after the bird regardless. It flew on, unscathed, until it was out of sight. This point was almost a carbon copy of our earlier one. "Good boy, Fergus, good boy," I said when he returned to the spot of the flush. I wrapped my arms around his deep chest and kissed him on the head. He wriggled out of my dog hug, wanting nothing to do with such foolishness out in the field.

We cut the trail shortly and started the walk back toward the truck, my mind on autopilot as Fergus continued to worry the cover on both sides of the trail, constantly searching, always the optimist. A mile or so of walking brought us back past the Homestretch Patch, this time on the trail across its north side. I didn't really notice Fergus slipping into the cover here until I heard the silence of his bell. I scolded myself for not keeping better track of him as I daydreamed my way home, but I figured he was somewhere within the Homestretch. Given its small size, he couldn't be that hard to locate.

It took me a couple of minutes searching, but I found him pointing on the eastern edge of the cover adjacent to several neatly planted rows of red pine. Before I got up to the dog, a grouse burst out of the closest pines, and I watched it fly out of range. *There is another one. I hadn't subtracted the only bird.* I was so delighted and so relieved to find another bird left in the Homestretch Patch I never even considered shooting at it.

Ten days later, winter had clamped down on northern Wisconsin, dumping nearly a foot of snow and dropping the temperature below zero. This harsh weather effectively ended our grouse season, and I traded my shotgun for cross-country skis. About two weeks after shooting the bird in the Homestretch Patch, I found myself skiing past the very spot I had shot the bird, my last of the season, and I stopped next to the place where I thought I had taken the shot. I shortly found the fallen oak branch, the withered leaves now sheathed in snow and ice. No wonder the bird hunkered there—it was a cozy little spot, offering cover, even more so now with a coating of fluffy snow.

Standing there, I could still see Fergus turn his head slowly to the right and down until his nose pointed at the fallen oak branch. I could still see the bird flush into the sky and roll away from me before it fell. May I never forget that day, that bird.

An Iowa Cornfield and
the Wisconsin Woods

When he eased the Browning out of the case, he did so reverentially. "I like to carry this at least once a year," my friend said about the Superposed he was holding up for us to admire, a shotgun he inherited from his father. It was a fine gun, Belgian made, but you could tell from the shiny bluing and dings in the wood that his father hadn't pampered it. Envious, I have always wished I had inherited a shotgun from my father or a mentor, but I never had relationships of that kind growing up. "At least once a year," he said, wiping down the barrel with his gloved hand, "I like to bring it out."

Guns are regularly passed down to family and friends with little fanfare and no public record, but we have at least two stories in upland literature of such bequests. Charles Norris, author of *Eastern Upland Hunting*, gifted George Bird Evans a Purdey. Actually, he allowed Evans to pick from his guns when infirmity ended hunting for Norris. This gun, I'm told, has since passed into the hands of one of Evans's friends.

For thirty-four years, Evans had been shooting a Fox side-by-side, and figured he would go to his grave shooting that gun. "I've dreamed elaborate dreams about shooting, but that I would someday own and shoot a Purdey was not one of them," he wrote in "A Gun to Remember" in *The Upland Shooting Life*. The gun was a dream because of its cost—a new one today sets you back more than a Mercedes-Benz. Evans modified the 12 gauge, giving it more length, more drop, and more castoff, so it would fit him, and he carried and shot the English gun in his West Virginia coverts until his early eighties. In his last decade, Evans stopped shooting the Purdey and moved on to an AyA 28 gauge—a much lighter shotgun than the Purdey—a gun he describes in a posthumous article in *Pointing Dog Journal.*

Another lucky writer was William Tapply, who inherited Burton Spiller's old Parker 20 gauge and writes about this transaction in his story "Burt's Gun." One October day, while the young Tapply hunted with his father and Burt, Spiller asked to exchange guns with Tapply. Spiller took Tapply's single-shot Savage and put the Parker side-by-side in his young hands. At the end of the day, he took the single-shot when he got out of Tapply's dad's car, leaving young Bill with the Parker. "Thus did Burt Spiller's gun pass into my hands—in Burt's way, without ceremony, without giving me the chance to say 'thank you,' and therefore without his need to acknowledge that he indeed bestowed upon me a priceless gift," wrote Tapply. When Burt died in 1973, the Savage also came back to Tapply, so he ended up with two of Burt's guns technically. This Parker 20 gauge, by the way, was sold at auction in 2008 and was described as a shotgun owned by two "high priests of grouse hunting."

Like Tapply, my first shotgun was also a single-shot Savage, but in 12 gauge, which I bought in dilapidated shape from a high school buddy for ten dollars. I brought it back to life as a shop-class project, which amazes me today in this age of school shootings. Granted, that old 12 gauge was a breech-breaking single shot and not a semiautomatic rifle or a handgun capable of multiple killings, but it was nevertheless a lethal weapon. Given our changed attitudes toward guns and the shootings that seem to occur routinely, no school administration would okay this shop project in today's climate. It was a different world back then.

With that gun, I shot my first pheasant, my first woodcock, and my first grouse, but for some reason I traded it in on my first over-and-under. I was young and didn't think much about tradition when I did so. Only with hindsight do I recognize that gun's significance in my hunting. The fifty dollars I got in trade has long since disappeared, but I'm glad to have the memories of the birds I shot with it.

In small-town Iowa in the seventies, a kid with a gun was considered normal, and maybe she or he still is in some parts. I hope so. In the fall, I used to roam the hills and valleys around my hometown with my brother or my buddy Phil. Occasionally, we used our bicycles to increase our predatory range, and my first .22 (also a single shot) still has gouges on the forearm piece where I rested it on the handlebar while we bounced down gravel roads.

Once or twice a year, we would actually get in a car to do our hunting, driving ten or twenty miles to the west, where there were more pheasants as the Mississippi River hills and valleys gave way to a more rolling prairie. A few times I went with a friend and his dad, and we would slowly drive Iowa gravel roads scanning the ditches for roosters while his dad drank Budweisers, what I would call today a booze cruise. We missed a lot of birds, but every so often my friend's dad would connect with a pheasant, and then we would scramble down into the ditch and maybe out into a picked cornfield running after a wounded bird. We were the dogs. If my parents knew my friend's dad was drinking and driving while taking us hunting, they didn't let on or looked the other way. I like to think they never knew what was going on.

I grew up in a world with considerably fewer technological distractions than today, and about the only thing competing with my hunting was playing football. We did have a TV, which pulled in two stations on the rabbit-ears antenna, but when I look back on the screen quality of analog it's a wonder we watched TV at all. It was usually like watching TV in a blizzard. Most of our information came from newspapers and magazines. We had a telephone, but long-distance calls were so dear, we used it only for local calls and the occasional timed long-distance call. My freshman year in college, I didn't talk to my parents from the start of the fall semester until I came home for Thanksgiving break, although both of my parents regularly wrote me letters—unheard of today. I know because I have asked my students. Many can't manage a simple email, let alone a handwritten letter.

Today, screens surround us. We have them in all the rooms of our houses, in our purses, briefcases, and backpacks. We look at them in our vehicles, frequently while driving. We even take them with us out hunting, sometimes in case we get bored, more often for communication or information. My students tell me they surf the internet or Facebook while in the deer stand. The distractions for today's children are legion, and it's no wonder fewer and fewer kids are spending time in nature and more specifically hunting. Nature on a screen is much more accessible, exciting, and consumable than the real thing in regular slow time. A lot of time passes between grouse flushed on most days. On a TV show, the host and guest can shoot a limit of birds in about fifteen minutes, and those guys never miss.

Rampant urbanization has also contributed to the decline in hunting. Both my parents and my wife's parents grew up on small farms, mine in Wisconsin, hers in southwest Iowa. Later, when they had married, both couples settled in small Iowa towns and took white-collar jobs. Each of us, however, grew up in a house about one block from the country, from the start of the woods and cornfields surrounding our towns. We had the luxury of access to the land that many kids growing up in metropolitan areas don't have. Where does a kid living in New York, Chicago, Houston, L.A. go to hunt?

Divorce also complicates this issue. Our neighbor kids often come down to our yard when Fergus and Jenkins are out and ask if they can play with them. Once in a while, they knock on the door and ask if they can lead them around the yard, so we clip the dogs to leashes and let them ramble around the yard. The boy who lived next door particularly loved to play with them because he didn't have a dog of his own. I promised to take him grouse and woodcock hunting when he passed hunter safety.

One Saturday afternoon he happened into our yard just as I pulled in from a hunt. I had shot a couple of grouse. I fanned out the gray tail on one of the birds and showed him the bulging crop, the ruff on its neck. "Can I carry one?" he asked. His eyes visibly widened when I handed him a bird by a leg. He took it in hand like he was handling a precious vase. Previous to this, he was interested mostly in deer hunting, but a ruffed grouse in hand had planted a seed.

His parents divorced shortly thereafter, and then his mom took a job in Texas and moved their kids there. Obviously, he won't get a chance to hunt grouse there, and given Texas and its lack of public hunting, there's little chance he'll get to hunt anything. His dad, who still lives next door, tells me he will be home for Thanksgiving and they plan to deer hunt together then. I hope so.

Today I roam the woods of Wisconsin with a gun I didn't even dare dream of owning as a kid—a Browning Superlight Feather. It's not as classy as Evans's Purdey or as storied as the Superposed my friend inherited from his father, but since it's a couple of pounds lighter, the gun is efficient in rough country where grouse and woodcock thrive. Right now, I don't have anyone in mind to pass this gun on to, not that I've thought about this much. I like to think I have many more hunting years ahead. What I would like to pass along instead of a shotgun or two to some deserving kid, however, is the tradition of grouse and woodcock hunting.

Even though I hunted with a shabby gun as a kid in a small town, I had a lot more going for me than most of today's youth interested in hunting. I had a place to hunt I could see and walk to from my front door. I had mentors willing to help and guide me along, despite some bad habits, and friends with whom to share hunts. I wasn't distracted by Facebook, Instagram, Snapchat, video games—the screens that dominate our daily lives.

They really were the good old days.

Legacy

On Hunting Public Land

had walked close to half a mile up the logging road through a recent aspen cutting. From the road, the cutting didn't look all that impressive, but more than halfway through it, I realized it was much larger than it looked from the road. It was at least five hundred acres, maybe larger. Still, we hadn't put up a single bird, not even a woodcock in all that promising cover. Fergus hadn't slowed his pace at all, indicating he had yet to cut any bird scent. Maybe it was too big, too much of a monoculture, since after all it was a pure stand of aspen. More likely it was still too young—the trees not much more than head high—and needed more time to age into fine grouse and woodcock habitat.

I had been driving by this chunk of public land on my way to and from other coverts for several years, paying it little mind. This corner of the county was mostly mature hardwoods, so I didn't take much notice of it as grouse and woodcock ground. It looked like most of the other woodlands in the area—good for furniture and firewood, but not so good for birds. Then, driving by one day, I noticed a couple of fresh clear-cuts and noted them on my map when I got home in the evening. Several years later, two of the clear-cuts thriving, I finally stopped to check out the place.

We were almost to the end of the cutting, clearly marked by the edge of mature hardwoods above the popple marching across the

A winter hunt among the aspen. (Susan Parman)

east-west boundary. The cover was a bust and needed to mature a few more seasons. The oaks and maples ahead towered above and dwarfed the spindly popples. Since I had walked all the way in, I decided I would follow this edge between the young and the old trees south back to the truck. It was a transition zone that grouse in particular frequented. Before coming to the edge, however, I discovered a jumpable creek meandering through the popple, bounded by Christmas-tree-size balsam fir. Another edge, this one in the midst of all that aspen. This looked good. A grouse hunter is always hunting for grousier cover, and this had that look. My predatory instinct kicked in.

The creek was less than a yard across where it cut a deep trench across the logging road. I could either skip across on a larger rock in the creek bed or take a flying leap across. I took a few steps back, then a couple of quick steps forward, and launched into the air, hoping to regain my high school long-jump form, even weighed down as I was with a hunting vest, shotgun, and heavy boots. At the peak of my jump, crazy as it sounds, I looked to my left and noticed Fergus, just on the other side of the creek, stopped and pointing, tail rigid and parallel to his back. Before I thudded to a landing, my brain registered POINT. When my boots hit the ground, three or four birds flushed up out of the popple and beat it toward the tree line. I took a few quick steps toward the dog, and two more birds shot up—one more or less in my direction. It was quartering away from me, and I caught up with the feathery rocket as it flew across the opening and out over the logging road, dropping it in the popple on the other side. Bird in hand, the day was already a success, and I mentally added this new covert to my list.

Ninety-nine percent of the land that grouse and woodcock hunters in Wisconsin hunt is public—county, state, and federal forest lands. Nearly 20 percent of Wisconsin's landmass is public land, most of it open to hunting, in all a total of more than six million acres, an area larger than the entire state of New Hampshire, another grouse-hunting state. For another comparison, in Iowa, where I grew up, only 2.8 percent of the state is publicly owned. The fertile, black soil is too valuable as farmland to remain in the public domain and was homesteaded, settled, and sold off a century and a half ago. Today, it is some of the most intensely cultivated land in the country. In other words, it's much better to be a grouse hunter in Wisconsin than a pheasant hunter in Iowa, and this lack of public land is why I wouldn't want to move back.

Wisconsin, along with Michigan and Minnesota (not coincidentally the states with the highest grouse flush rates), have the most public land in the Midwest. In the nineteenth century much of this public land was logged off, completely razed, and vacated. Next, farmers moved into the stump-filled landscape, but many went under and they, like the logging companies, moved on. Some of this forsaken land the counties took over as tax delinquent, while other public lands were purchased with Pittman-Robertson money.

In our age of partisan and gridlock politics, we might be shocked to learn that Congress ever crafted any meaningful legislation, like the Pittman-Robertson Act, known officially as the Federal Aid in Wildlife Restoration Act of 1937. Sponsored by Nevada senator Key Pittman and Virginia congressman Absalom Willis Robertson and signed by Franklin D. Roosevelt on September 2, 1937, this act took over an existing 11 percent tax on guns and firearms and mandated the funds be dispersed by the Secretary of the Interior to the states to be spent on wildlife research and management as well as land acquisition. To date, the act has raised over ten billion dollars, and one benefit of the gun-buying binge during the Obama administration has been the tax money generated. Every handgun, every 9mm Glock sold has raised money for conservation, much of it public land acquisition, an irony considering the antigovernment stance of some gun owners.

Pittman-Robertson is one reason that Americans have millions of acres of public land on which to hunt, for it provided the funding for the public land tapestry that men like Theodore Roosevelt, Gifford Pinchot, and George Bird Grinnell created. In 2016 Wisconsin received $32.8 million in Pittman-Robertson and Dingell-Johnson funds, the sport-fishing equivalent of Pittman-Robertson. "Everyone benefits from this program whether or not they hunt, fish or boat," said Tom Melius of the US Fish and Wildlife Service, which administers these funds. "In many cases the parks where we watch birds, the public trails we hike on and the wildlife we observe would not exist without the funding provided by hunters, shooters, anglers and boaters. The [program] is leaving a lasting legacy for our nation's outdoor heritage."

The American idea of public land for the landless is a radical idea. It means the landless don't have to beg or trespass if we want to hunt, fish, camp, or roam. We are all equals on public land, unlike in civilized society where power and privilege separate, and sun, rain, snow, and leaves fall on us in like shares. Grouse and woodcock cannot be bought and sold—legally the people of Wisconsin own them. On public land, they are earned through perseverance and skill or bestowed upon us through luck and chance. Privatizing public land, the millions of acres where we can hunt for the price of a hunting license, would disenfranchise the poor and landless and deprive them of a common resource.

The wealth of public land in Wisconsin is one of the main reasons we moved here from Iowa. We were sick of all the No Trespassing signs. Since moving, we have bought a bit of our own land, and all totaled, we "own" about eight acres of private land, but "own" has several meanings. For instance, I have difficulty using the term "own" for something that has existed for four billion years just because a piece of paper gives me title to it. I can chase people off it and build my house there, but can I really own it? Someday it will "own" me, the earth enfolding my corpse as I decompose back into the soil. The oaks and maples that have stood beside our house since it was built own it more than we do.

The first definition signifies ownership or possession and is used to indicate property or interest. It is a capitalist's definition. I own this book, this car, this dog, although owning a dog is not the same as owning a book or a car. The second definition, according to Merriam-Webster, is "used to specify a direct or immediate relationship." This is the definition of ownership Aldo Leopold used in his essay "The Land Ethic." His view of land "changed the role of *Homo sapiens* from conqueror of the land-community to plain member and citizen of it. It implies respect for his fellow-members, and also respect for the community as such."

The first definition gives owners the right to do whatever they see fit with their property. A landowner can cut down a forest to mine ore or gravel or drain a swamp to build a strip mall. With the proper permits, a landowner can store depleted uranium or build a garbage dump. He can throw up a fence and start a game preserve and keep all nonpaying clients off the grounds, privatizing the hunting for those who can afford to pay for it. This is increasingly the model for quail plantations and pheasant preserves, a pay-to-shoot state of affairs only the wealthy can afford.

When former vice president Dick Cheney shot fellow hunter Harry Whittington while quail hunting in Texas in 2006, the media focused on Cheney's cover-up story and how he violated basic gun safety: knowing what's beyond the target. What struck me about the event, however, was Cheney's hunting on the private fifty-thousand-acre Armstrong Ranch in a state with virtually no public hunting ground. This was hunting for the elite, in a country that supposedly prided itself on public hunting for all of its citizens. Yes, it was a new world order.

Unlike the main definition of "own," the second denotes kinship, connection, and empathy. Leopold takes it further to include community, of which we are members. This does not mean we cannot use or shape the land, because we cannot help doing so either directly or indirectly. The second definition does not preclude our cutting of trees or taking of animals. If we use land, we will change it. Leopold did both on his Sauk County property. Even though he loved to study ruffed grouse and woodcock and provided habitat for them on his land, this didn't stop him from hunting them avidly.

More important, the capitalistic definition of "own" perceives land in strictly economic terms, and very short-term ones at that. If the iron ore beneath the oaks and maples is worth more than the trees growing on top, then woods are razed and sold for whatever the market will bear and we rip out the metal, leaving the land blasted and useless for years. Leopold notes that most members of the land community have little or no economic value, like trillium and wood thrushes. If a thing cannot be sold, this definition says it has no value. In this sense of the word, we don't even factor in the economic benefits of water retention, the carbon dioxide reduction from tree respiration, or the therapeutic value of the forest for those who walk in the woods. As long as we value land strictly in dollars, we will continue to abuse our property to reap whatever dollars we can wring from it.

Lately there have been increasing calls to privatize public lands, particularly in the western states, where public land makes up the majority of land in some states. Wisconsin has also reacted to this movement and started to sell off state lands. Much of the ideology behind this movement comes from the American Legislative Exchange Council (ALEC), a privately funded think tank that crafts legislation for Republican lawmakers. ALEC would love to free up public land for mining, timbering, and ranching interests, all the while preaching the benefits to the public. Their model legislation is called the Disposal and Taxation of Public Lands Act. At the 2016 Republican National Convention, a provision to hand public lands back to states went essentially unnoticed amid all the hoopla: "Congress shall immediately pass universal legislation providing for a timely and orderly mechanism requiring the federal government to convey certain federally controlled public lands to states. . . . The residents of state and local communities know best how to protect the land where they work and live," the RNC wrote.

The term "disposal" says a lot, treating land right up there with junk TVs, dirty motor oil, and used coffee filters. Of course, this legislation touts the benefits to the public, such as more jobs and more local tax revenue, but essentially it would "dispose" of any citizen's right to use public lands, not to mention the rights of the indigenous plants and animals. This fire sale of public land would affect not just hunters but also hikers, skiers, campers, fishers, mountain bikers, berry pickers, horseback riders, and mushroom gatherers. In short, such legislation trades the rights of the many for the profits of the few.

The shame and panic I felt as a kid approaching an Iowa farmer and asking permission to hunt pheasants on his land still burn in my mind. We feared this job, so we would flip a coin to see who had to slump up to the door hat in hand and beg for permission. Some of the farmers were kind, others mean and gruff. One old curmudgeon, who had plastered his land with large No Trespassing signs, sat at his picture window with binoculars during pheasant season. Dozens of times we flushed flocks of pheasants over his barbwire fence and past the old tire painted No Hunting hanging on his fence. Oh, how I wanted to turn poacher every time that happened. I'm surprised I never took a shot at the tire. In Iowa, unless pheasant hunters own or lease land, both requiring a fair amount of money, they are reduced to begging for permission. Not so in Wisconsin, where grouse and woodcock hunters have access to millions of acres. Here, the free can freely hunt.

On the drive home, I found myself humming Woodie Guthrie's song "This Land Is Your Land." As I did, I thought about what to name this new and delightful covert. Leaping Creek first came to mind, or Jump Creek, but by the time I had pulled into the drive, with Fergus curled up on the passenger seat and snoring ever so slightly, I had settled on Legacy.

Later that evening, I Googled the lyrics to Guthrie's song. I didn't know the words, other than the chorus, which is why I was humming on the way home. I found out there were two versions—the official and the original—and I knew of only the official 1944 version. This version struck out two verses Guthrie wrote in 1940, including one questioning the fencing and posting of private property. I thought about calling the new covert Woodie Guthrie's Legacy, but that was too much of a mouthful. It would simply be Legacy. A gift to all—our inheritance, our right, our legacy.

Red Bud Road

Banding Woodcock

After I tied Fergus to a slim birch tree twenty yards behind us, I went back to where we had flushed the hen woodcock. Crouching down, it took me less than a minute to find the first chick about an arm's length away, only its quick breathing faintly visible. It looked like a fuzzy tennis ball, its bumblebee-like camouflage highly effective against dusty yellow and darker grays of fallen aspen and birch leaves.

From his tree, Fergus watched with interest as I scanned the ground for the remaining three chicks. Tom Goltz, the master bander supervising my first banding efforts, worked a larger circle around me, also looking for the rest of the chicks. With the color pattern of the first chick etched into my mind, I found numbers two and three in short order, and both were within my reach, frozen where they sat.

I felt sorry for these chicks in a way, sorry to disturb their peace, but I understood the valuable information their bands might someday provide about their age, habits, and movements, the habitat they frequent, as well as general population trends. They were cute little buggers, and we quickly determined they were three days old (aged by beak length, in this case 21 mm). They were surprisingly docile even when picked up and seemed to trust us. By the time we started

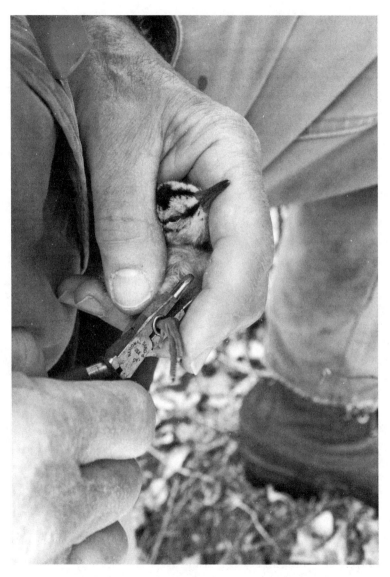

Tom Goltz bands a three-day-old woodcock chick. (Mark Parman)

banding, however, the nervous hen began working back toward us and her helpless and, she thought, endangered chicks. She was upwind from us, and Fergus was at the end of his rope, nostrils twitching, pointing her once again.

We searched for the last chick only a few more minutes, so as not to unduly stress out the family, and then, after measuring all their bills, we quickly banded all three chicks. Since a newly hatched chick's foot is large enough to prevent the aluminum band from slipping off its leg (about half size at birth), it's possible to band chicks just days old. Woodcock chicks begin to fly at twelve days, making them considerably more difficult to capture, so getting them before flight is the most effective technique.

With the last chick banded, Tom sculpted a shallow nest in the leaves wherein he placed the chicks, I unleashed Fergus from his tree, and we quickly and silently retreated. The hen would be back safe and united—and no doubt relieved—with her brood a few minutes later.

On the way out of the cover, Fergus pointed two more woodcock—one an adult male, the other a chick that could fly. While he was pointing, we located a second chick, but it flushed out of Tom's grasp when he tried to grab it. These chicks, roughly two weeks old, were two-thirds full grown and flying strongly. In a month's time, it would be difficult to tell this year's chicks from an adult woodcock.

The Wisconsin DNR cannot afford to fully fund its research projects on white-tailed deer, wolves, black bear, or turkeys, species with much higher social profiles than the lowly woodcock. In fact, on Earth Day of 2015—on a day when I was searching for broods—Governor Scott Walker announced he was cutting sixty-six DNR environmental jobs. The irony was not lost on anyone paying attention. Another former Wisconsin governor, Gaylord Nelson, instituted Earth Day in the 1970s. On the other hand, a few years back Governor Walker had no problem spending well over $100,000 to hire a private deer czar to review the DNR's approach to deer management.

The Wisconsin DNR, like the other wildlife agencies in the upper Midwest, cannot afford to conduct large-scale woodcock banding operations. Their wildlife biologists are swamped with other responsibilities. Many state employees would love to spend their workdays in the spring woods—among the trillium and rue anemone, with the roll of a drumming grouse in the distance—banding woodcock. This might be how many envisioned their work for the agency, out in the field conducting research, but they spend much of their time on more mundane tasks. Our wildlife agencies are strapped for funds and cannot afford the latest technology, the miniature GPS units attached to woodcock so they can be live-tracked via satellite. Since most agencies cannot afford the manpower or technology to do proper woodcock research, they must rely on help from lay individuals, experienced hunters with trained pointing dogs.

Not only are we defunding science; many today are skeptical of its results, especially when they clash with our individual beliefs and opinions. It's not just some of our politicians who mistrust science today; the average American does not put much faith in scientists. A Pew study, "Public and Scientists' Views on Science and Society," published in January 2015, revealed the gap existing between what America's scientists and its citizens believe to be true of science-related issues. Here are some examples of the gap between the views of scientists and those of the public: belief in evolution, 98 percent of scientists versus 65 percent of the population; human activity as the primary cause of climate change, 87 percent to 50 percent; overpopulation as a major problem, 82 percent to 59 percent.

The study also found that "79 percent of adults say that science has made life easier for most people and a majority is positive about science's impact on the quality of health care, food and the environment." We like our iPhones, the power and speed of our vehicles, and the antibiotics keeping bacteria from infecting our bodies. We love how technology makes our lives easier, safer, more comfortable, and luxurious. What would we do without the internet, indoor plumbing, and the refrigerator?

One of the most intriguing sentences in the study: "Perceptions of where the scientific community stands on both climate change and evolution tend to be associated with individual views on the issue." In other words, we often do not allow science to challenge or change our individual subjective views. We believe what we want to believe, science be damned. This extends from hot-button issues like climate change and evolution to wildlife issues. If your scientist doesn't tell you what you want to hear, hire another scientist or a pseudoscientist. Better yet, believe what you want to believe.

In 2015 a research group led by Donald Waller, a professor of botany at the University of Wisconsin–Madison, showed that white-tailed deer "account for at least 40 percent of the change seen in the forests over the last half-century or so." Where deer are abundant, many nonnative plants have proliferated; meanwhile deer have munched their way through native trees, such as the sugar maple and other smaller shrubs. White-tails have also reduced the height of forest understory plants and decreased the number of flowering plants not woody or grassy. In other words, a white-tail deer herd that's larger than the land's carrying capacity significantly alters Northwoods habitat, reduces seedling shrubs and trees, and creates parklike landscapes.

Deer hunters naturally want to see as many deer as possible, and when they don't see multiple deer, they often blame other factors rather than their own hunting skills or blind luck: the DNR, wolves, baiters, poachers, other greedy hunters. But the landscape can carry only so many deer—the environmental-carrying capacity. This is often much lower than the social-carrying capacity—those deer hunters and even other wildlife watchers wanting to see massive herds of deer despite their negative effects on the landscape. Deer are a joy to watch and good to eat, so it's an understandable desire. But science tells us a lower number of deer makes for a healthier land, and in time an overall healthier herd. Too many deer will eat their way through their habitat, and the population will ultimately crash. The DNR must walk a razor's edge—keeping hunters happy while trying to maintain a healthy herd and healthy habitat.

Grouse hunters can also think subjectively about science. One of the debates in ruffed-grouse-hunting circles is the theory of hunting's compensatory or additive morality. In other words, does human predation of grouse affect population levels? Common sense would tell us a grouse removed from the woods is one less grouse. Aldo Leopold recognized in *Sand County Almanac* that a ruffed grouse embodied just a millionth of the energy of an acre in northern Wisconsin. But when a grouse is killed and removed, Leopold explained, the woods is utterly changed, much of its life force drained away. A grouse removed from the landscape does, to me, affect the soul or essence of that particular piece of ground. This subtraction could mean a vacant drumming log or a deafening silence after a day in the woods. But how does my hunting affect the overall population?

Years ago, I remember slumping out of the woods from one of my most productive covers, a long trek of close to four hours at the height of October, and we hadn't put up a single grouse. At the parking lot, we ran into the game warden. "How'd it go?" he asked, after rolling down the window of his truck. "Nothing. I didn't see or hear a thing," I answered. I must have looked as depressed as I felt because he asked no more questions, and while I was coaxing the dog into the truck's box, he waved and drove off down the highway. True, it was a down year in the cycle, but I had busted some prime cover in one of my favorite coverts and not even heard a grouse flush. Yes, the emotive power of a single grouse had been lost.

George Bird Evans had a long-running battle with the West Virginia DNR over hunting seasons he considered too long (from the first of October to the end of February). The lengthy season he felt contributed to declining numbers of birds. In *An Affair with Grouse*, he wrote that years ago hunting pressure had little effect on grouse numbers—"the source of the false promise that gun pressure has no effect today." But as he aged and had accumulated fifty grouse seasons, he changed his mind on hunting pressure and overshooting grouse. "You can forget the tale about the grouse you don't shoot will die anyway," he wrote, meaning that a goshawk, owl, or fox will get it. Later he says, "You dare not shoot-out covers."

This notion that gunning has no effect on grouse numbers (the compensatory mortality hypothesis) was first advocated in 1935 by P. L. Errington and F. Hamerstrom, and ever since, the compensatory mortality theory has been at the heart of numerous studies and debates, and considered gospel by grouse hunters who want to justify shooting as many birds as possible. Gardiner Bump et alia also concluded in their seminal study, *The Ruffed Grouse: Life History, Propagation, Management*, that human predation was a minor component in ruffed-grouse-population dynamics. In other words, to most hunters and game departments, we could shoot as many birds as we wanted, so game departments extended seasons and increased bag limits, which is good for license sales. Grouse were like white pine—we could never cut them all down. They would last forever.

Later studies have shown that human predation can be additive, that overgunning does hurt the overall population of ruffed grouse. In 1984 John Kubisiak found that a mean harvest rate of 44 percent or above was additive to natural mortality and reduced Wisconsin ruffed grouse densities. Further studies in Wisconsin showed human predation did, in fact, affect ruffed grouse numbers. We know this is true in "our own" coverts because we know they can be shot out; otherwise, we wouldn't call them coverts, and we wouldn't keep them secret. They are "ours" and we wish to protect them and keep them to ourselves. In some cases, if they're going to be shot out, we want to do the shooting. Deep down, we know it can happen.

In the field, conditions vary widely, complexity rules the day, and much remains unknown. Nature is not stable like a laboratory, making it difficult to replicate conditions in the woods to gain consistent results for studies. We can't even figure out why grouse populations cycle regularly about every ten years. We need more data, more studies, which is why I want to continue banding woodcock.

But more than anything, hunters must realize that science is not going to tell to us what we want to hear (that we can shoot unlimited numbers of grouse or that deer should be as common as sparrows); it is not meant to tickle our itching ears. Science is in the business of getting at facts and winnowing the truth, whether the facts or the truth is agreeable or disagreeable. Like the guiding principle of the University of Wisconsin, science should remain relentless in its pursuit of the truth, regardless of how that truth affects us.

It's late October nearing the end of woodcock season, and I've stolen out of work for a short afternoon hunt. Jenkins is just a pup, and after some early success in his first season, he has turned to chasing birds rather than pointing them, so I have brought him out to the county forest to hunt right off Red Bud Road, where there should be woodcock. I know because we banded them the previous spring. For sure, other hunters have been through here by this late in the season — after all, this cover sits right on the road, advertising itself like a billboard to any passing upland hunter, but I'm counting on some being left.

Twenty yards off the road, Jenkins starts to make game and eases into a point, and when he goes solid, I look in front of his nose for the bird. "Easy, boy," I whisper. "Easy." But before I get around him, Jenkins lunges forward, up twitters the bird, and we both watch it fly batlike up and over the young popple.

"Jenkins," I growl, "whoa. You whoa." I pick him up by the collar and his hind end and carry him back to the spot where he first hit scent and stopped. "*Whoa!*" Normally soft, he shoots his eyes at me, then back at the scent. He looks as though his crime was worth the punishment. I kick leaves and sticks around in front of him, daring him to flinch. I come around behind him and push his hindquarters, but he remains staunch, so I tap him on the head and turn him loose. "Okay, hunt 'em up."

In short order, we repeat the same dance—Jenkins pointing and flushing, me setting him up and growling him out. After his second bust, I find the control unit for his e-collar in my vest pocket. I don't want to use it, but I don't want to see a third strike. Making sure it's on the lowest level, I hold my finger over the red On button as he works for the next woodcock.

Jenkins finds a third woodcock in short order, still within sight of Red Bud Road. This time, I spot the bird two yards in front of Jenkins. Without thinking, I drop the control unit back into my pocket and walk in quickly before Jenkins has much of a chance to flush the woodcock. This time, *I* flush it. The woodcock twitters up through the popple as I track it with my shotgun. When it clears the trees, instead of pulling the trigger I say, "Bang." Jenkins breaks with the flush and stops twenty yards ahead, watching the bird fly off.

Most likely, we had banded this bird in April. Those fluffy little chicks had trusted me with their lives in the spring, and they seemed to still. I couldn't pull the trigger on a trust like that.

Swamp Loop

Just a Thimble of Meat

J enkins, after some coaxing, dropped the russet-colored bird into
my hand. It was a large bird, as far as woodcock go. It had some
heft to it, so it was likely a female—generally up to 20 percent heavier
than a male. When I compared it with the other woodcock we had
shot a few minutes earlier, the size difference was obvious. Still, as
game birds go, the woodcock is on the small end, about the same size
as a bobwhite quail. It is the smallest game animal we shoot and eat.
An average white-tailed deer provides a hundred times as much meat
as the woodcock. I slid both birds back into my game bag and started
off in Jenkins's direction.

Cornell University's birding website, eBird, recently posted a
piece about the annual woodcock wingbee the US Fish and Wildlife
Service holds each spring, where volunteers count, record, and study
the thousands of woodcock wings that hunters mail in. Susan and I
send in our wings, placing them in the envelopes provided by the
USFWS, recording time and place of kill, and mailing them off.
Many of these wings come from woodcock who haunt a covert we
call the Swamp Loop. All these wings give wildlife biologists their
best picture of woodcock population dynamics and trends.

In the comments section of this website I read the posting of a
woman who was "thankful" scientists were studying the woodcock

population, but wondered why anyone would want to shoot such a small, defenseless bird. "After all, it is just a thimble of meat."

She was right, woodcock offer a scant amount of meat. But thimble? They're more like a shot glass of meat than a thimble. At six ounces dressed, they're about the same size as a mourning dove and have a similar taste. In some of our recipes, these game birds are interchangeable. For a social get-together, we once fixed mourning doves, employing a rumaki recipe we use for woodcock. We told those gathered we had made "woodcock rumaki" because we felt some might have been offended eating the bird of peace, the bird showing up at their feeders. Some of the guests had eaten our woodcock rumaki before, and yet none detected the imposter mourning doves.

If I'm following it correctly, the woman's argument runs such: Since the woodcock is such a small bird, why bother hunting it? Why kill this beautiful bird when it offers so little food? According to her, it's morally defensible to kill and eat larger animals, who offer more bang for the buck, or in this case more meat for the shell.

Size of the animal was once a consideration, particularly before agribusiness and factory farming made meat so cheap to purchase and widespread on our tables. In the days when many Americans hunted for meat, say before 1940, most shells were expensive and treated like rare treasures, with the exception of .22 ammo, but then one could not hit a woodcock with a .22 unless one could shoot like Annie Oakley, who reportedly could shatter small glass balls thrown in the air with her .22 pistol. Even a squirrel has significantly more meat than a woodcock, not to mention a rabbit, a pheasant, or a duck. These bigger bodies were worth shooting with more expensive shells.

But this woman wasn't worried about burning powder and wasting shot. She was opposed to hunting a tiny bird and, in her opinion, a defenseless one. Having missed hundreds of woodcock over the years, I can only conclude they are not defenseless. On a grouse and woodcock hunt, my brother and a friend once burned through two boxes of ammo and then all the shells I had left in my hunting vest when we ran into one of the heaviest concentrations of woodcock flight birds I have ever witnessed in Wisconsin. They killed only a pair of birds with the shells in their pockets. We had to drive to the nearest town to buy more shells. In defense of their skills, my brother and friend hailed from central Iowa and were used to shooting pheasants—big-bodied birds that usually flushed in the clear skies of an Iowa slough or cornfield. That's much different from shooting a dinking and juking bird flying through tag alders and aspen thickets, which is sometimes like trying to shoot in a phone booth (remember those?). Woodcock may hold well for a pointing dog, and not flush in a way that unhinges a shooter, but they are still not easy shots.

The woodcock's ability to sit tight in its camouflaging feathers conceals its presence to hunters, especially those without dogs. When my dogs point woodcock, I often search in front of their noses for the bird, which is typically within five or so yards of the dog. Sometimes, I give up trying to find the bird and wade in for the flush in front of the dog. I can't tell you how many times the woodcock comes up right where I was looking for it. Like many prey animals, their feathers have evolved to blend into their habitat, their coffee and russet colors matching the carpet of leaves, twigs, and duff of the floor of a Northwoods forest. No, they have developed significant defenses, else they would have been killed off long ago.

But back to the "bigger is better" argument. It would follow then that I should be hunting turkeys or Canada geese. Or even more defensible, deer or elk. Elephant maybe? I imagine, however, the woman would have also opposed the hunting of elephants, maybe on the grounds they were so large and majestic or exotic and endangered.

I do understand part of this woman's argument, however, and as I age, find myself agreeing more often with her sentiments, not that this makes them right. The woodcock *is* a cute and dainty creature. Having witnessed its sky dance in the spring, I limit my shooting and take a bird or two instead of the daily bag limit of three. Like Aldo

Leopold, one of our first wildlife biologists, I don't want my shooting to upset the delicate balance of the sky dance. When these reflective moments strike, I flush the bird and watch it fly off, but on other days, I have no problem filling my daily limit.

It's hard for me to explain these conflicting ideas and emotions, the contradiction within myself. Some days, I can pull the trigger with impunity; other days it's as if my trigger finger is frozen. On those days, I might as well enter the woods with a broomstick. I've tried to analyze my situation. Is it related to the weather, my age, lack of sleep, working a young dog needing woodcock experience, the reinforcement of a bird-in-hand? Was it the latent effect of watching *Bambi* as a kid, Walt Disney's popular philosophy? Has the banding of woodcock, holding a cute, fluffy day-old chick in my hands, feeling it tremble and pulse with life—had that spoiled my appetite for their deaths? From wherever these notions have arisen, it's clear they have made me at times one fickle hunter.

In analyzing the killing I have done, I realize these thoughts arise nearly every time I come upon a just-killed animal. The still clear eye of the doe lying in the snow. The rooster crumpled, head beneath its wing, and crashed into the stubble of a picked cornfield. The ruffed grouse breast up, beating its wings in the debris of the forest floor in one last effort to evade me, the predator. There is often a moment when I want to throw the dying or dead bird into the air and say, "Arise, waken, and fly away," but I have no powers of resurrection and must live with what I have done. Do other hunters have these same thoughts, or can they simply pull the trigger with no regrets? I envy my dogs, whose instinct so overpowers them at the moment of the kill; they think of nothing else save the capture of game. Their prey drive overrides all.

John Keats famously called the ability to deal with these inner contradictions "negative capability, that is, when a man is capable of being in uncertainties, mysteries, doubts, without any irritable reaching after fact and reason." It is, and will always be, a mystery to me how

I can say I love an animal and yet be the cause of its destruction. I can see and feel many of the arguments of the animal rights movement. I do have an intellectual problem with pain, especially when I am the agent of it. C. S. Lewis wrote that the world was designed so life can continue "only by preying upon one another. In the lower forms this process entails only death, but in the higher there appears a new quality called consciousness which enables it to be attended with pain." He went on to say we "live by inflicting pain"—and, it goes without saying, death. I don't think, though, that Lewis ever hunted.

We worked through the cover without another point. When we hit the next intersection, I could choose the direct route back to the truck or head east out of the swamp and bushwhack up a ridge where we had put up woodcock before in a tiny patch of aspen. I called Jenkins, and he followed as I headed into the brush and up the ridge.

A few birds were still using this cover, we found out quickly once we arrived. Their fresh whitewash was splashed on leaves and sere grass, the occasional twig. The first bird Jenkins pointed lay beneath a head-high bush still bearing its leaves, the only green in this aspen stand. When the bird twittered up, I was in the middle of the bush trying to see through the screen of leaves. I fired once at the bird's silhouette and missed, and held off on the second barrel as the bird bored straight through the popple, more like a grouse than a woodcock.

We were nearly out of the cover when Jenkins slowed and hunkered nose down into a point. He had nailed another. This bird, on the edge of the cutting, flushed out into the relative open of the mature oaks, and the widely spaced trees offered a much easier shot. I dropped it in a puff of feathers. The bird was still alive, head up, its large eye boring into mine when I took it from Jenkins. Quickly without thought, I dispatched it by breaking its neck.

Jenkins noses a late season woodcock. (Susan Parman)

I had not been thinking about the problem of pain since we had started up this ridge. Maybe the gloom of the swamp had darkened my thoughts down below in the murk and dampness. Up here on the ridge, things were much brighter, much clearer. I could see a few miles from up here.

Swanda's

Late July—the evening was clear but humid, the air heavy and smelling of summer. An out-of-state grouse-hunting friend called to chat and mentioned how early the upcoming grouse season started, September 12. "For me, the season doesn't really start until October 1," he said. By then with any luck, he hoped, the temperatures would have cooled and some of the leaves fallen. I agreed with him: October 1 feels more like grouse season, while early grouse season often has an August-like feel.

As we talked, I realized that the last time the grouse season opened on September 12, Fergus was seven months old almost to the day. Just seven green months old. We had lost both of our veteran hunters in the past year, and he was our only dog. I looked at his lanky and awkward teenage body and said, "Well, you're it, Ferg. You're all we have. Are you ready?" Even though he had no idea what I was saying, he thumped his skinny tail on the wood floor.

I told my friend this over the phone, recounting the two birds I shot over Fergus that opening day when he was a puppy really. It was a hot and humid September 12, and we quit before ten—sweat beads dripping in my eyes, my pants sticking to my legs. I couldn't accurately recall the best parts: Fergus's points, the shots, holding the birds in my hands and letting Fergus get a whiff of his first birds. I couldn't pull up that film from my archives. "Well, buddy, you should have written it down," my friend said.

After I hung up, I remembered I had recorded that day. I found my hunting journal for 2009 on the bookshelf and leafed through it for my opening day entry. Good for me—it was a fairly long entry. In fact, I had written a note the Friday night before with the joy and anticipation of a kid on Christmas Eve:

Sept. 11—well, tomorrow is the grouse opener, and it will be my first season since 1995 w/out Gunnar or Ox, so it will be a bitter-sweet experience to be out in the woods w/ Fergus. He has regressed and has started busting birds. The good news is that he's birdy and loves to hunt. Fergus, though, is only 7 months old today.

I then pulled out Fergus's papers. He was born on February 11, so he was exactly seven months and one day old on the opener. That entry brought back even more memories, of training Fergus in late summer. For a while we were justifiably worried about him because he wouldn't bust any thick cover, particularly blackberry brambles. He walked behind us, stepping on our heels. I wondered if he had any prey drive and thought it was going to be one very long season, but I needn't have worried, for today Fergus ranges far and wide, sometimes too far, especially when we are in wolf country. His prey drive pushes him to the outer limits of my concerns and fears.

My journal evoked a recollection of the first grouse he ever pointed while we were out on Swanda's land training for the upcoming season. I have trained all my dogs here in this covert. It's close to home, and it reliably holds birds, both ruffed grouse and woodcock. A creek bordered by tag alders meanders through the property. It's easy to get around on the maze of logging roads through the maturing aspen. Here I shot Gunnar's first ruffed grouse, a large gray bird whose tail is framed and still hangs in our hallway. A quarter of a mile from this bird, I shot a grouse over Ox with my first over-and-under, my first "real" grouse and woodcock gun. Swanda's has layers and layers of memories, which is another reason that I keep returning.

Back to Fergus. Here he pointed and held the first grouse he ever encountered. I could see it up ahead, skulking away from us, and I prayed Fergus would stay steady as I hurried around to corral the bird and flush it. My pincer movement worked. I got around it and flushed it before Fergus broke. It popped up out of the tag alders and planed across the creek. I yelled, "Fergus, you did it. You're such a good boy. I can't believe you did it." He barreled over to me and jumped into my arms. I started to cry, joy tears. Here's my journal from that day:

> Aug. 19—Hunted Swanda's. Fergus pointed his first grouse out, maybe blood kin to the last bird I shot over Ox. It was also about 100 yards from the first bird I ever shot over Ox. The circle continues.

I flipped back a few pages and found the entry for Ox's last bird, as my 2008 hunting journal was also in this notebook. It was a Thursday, right before the start of the gun deer season. Because of deer season, we wouldn't hunt for almost two weeks. When the grouse flushed, it made the mistake of crossing over the logging road, and I shot it there, the wad sticking into its breast, the only time I have ever had that happen. Had I known that to be the last ruffed grouse I would ever shoot over Ox, I would have wept like a schoolgirl. It's best not to know some things. I probably would have kept that burnt and bloody wad as well.

My journal entry for September 12, Fergus's first official outing, is uncharacteristically long, so I'll condense. We first ran into a woodcock, not legal game until the following weekend. Fergus pointed the first woodcock, but before I could get to him he broke his point and bumped it. Then he bumped the second woodcock, and I had started to despair, wondering if he would ever get it. He pointed a third woodcock, and I got around him and flushed this one. It twittered up into the sky as I tracked it with the barrel of my shotgun. "*Pow!*" I yelled for Fergus's benefit. Mine, too.

Fergus, among the aspen, points a ruffed grouse, front leg raised in a classic pose. (Susan Parman)

In the next cover, Fergus again pointed. I marched in promptly, silently praying he would hold, and a covey of young birds exploded all around me like shrapnel, flushing frantically in all four directions. One grouse flew up into a low branch of a nearby aspen. The three-quarter-sized bird looked down at us thinking it was safe from the wingless predators below. Fergus, staring up at the perching bird, was trembling with excitement and so was I. His nose was twitching as he sought out the bird's scent. I whispered, "Whoa," and slowly moved toward the bird, the stock of my shotgun in my armpit. The bird jumped into the air, I dumped it a couple of feet from its perch, and Fergus was on it. Some hunters might not shoot birds that flush out of trees, but I was determined to get that first ruffed grouse for Fergus.

The second bird on that warm opening day was a lucky shot, but much more conventional. Fergus pointed, and I flushed it and shot into a wall of green where I thought the bird would be, tracking it by sound. The shot string tore through leaves and branches. It's a wonder any shot could get through all of that vegetation and find the bird, but I stood still and heard its wings drumming their last beat on woods debris. Fergus had bird number two on his first day of grouse hunting. The last sentence of the entry: "We got out of the woods at 10 a.m. and it was nearly seventy." I also wanted to quit while we were ahead, end on a high note.

A few years after this, I found a photo from that first hunt, one I thought was lost when my computer unexpectedly crashed. I had saved it on a thumb drive, stashed and forgotten in the back of a cluttered desk drawer. In it, I'm posing in the backyard in shorts, T-shirt, and flip-flops, holding two juvenile birds next to Fergus. He has a goofy juvenile look on his face. The leaves on the backyard trees are summer green; there's not a bit of color, a hint of fall. Fergus is skinny and lanky, with little of the silky feathering characteristic of a mature setter. He looks twenty pounds lighter than he is today, his frame not yet filled out. I look younger too.

I don't know if anyone except me will ever read my hunting journals or even if anyone would care to. They are a ragtag collection of notebooks and paper-clipped sheets of paper. They look like they need to be thrown out, but if the house were on fire, they might be the first thing I would grab as we fled. No, I would grab them second. The dogs would go first.

Transylvania

As a kid, I raced home from school on my Sears and Roebuck bike so I could catch the TV series *Dark Shadows*. If I got home quickly enough, I could pour a glass of milk and grab a couple of graham crackers before the show started. Oh, the thrill when the vampire fluttered open his eyes and rose up out of his wooden coffin, white fangs gleaming. I read Bram Stoker's *Dracula* cover to cover in about a day, even though it was not required reading for class, and I watched every vampire movie the nineteenth-century novel inspired. I especially loved the reruns of the Bela Lugosi movies every time they aired on the Saturday night Creature Feature. I even dressed up as Count Dracula for Halloween and begged my parents to buy me Count Chocula cereal. As an adult, I didn't miss Keanu Reeves in *Bram Stoker's Dracula* and Will Smith in *I Am Legend*.

This was all before Lyme disease surfaced in Connecticut and spread to the Midwest. Lyme was followed by other tick-borne diseases—anaplasmosis (formerly known as a strain of ehrlichiosis) and now the Powassan virus, which might be the most insidious of all. Between 2006 and 2015, the Centers for Disease Control reported only sixteen cases of Powassan in Wisconsin and another twenty in Minnesota. These numbers of cases are extremely low compared with Lyme and anaplasmosis cases, but the Powassan is a virus with no known cure or vaccination, and it is much more deadly than the more common tick-borne bacterial infections.

As my knowledge of tick-borne disease increased, my enthusiasm for vampires waned. Walking out of the woods covered in deer ticks will do this. I never did get into the *Twilight* stuff, because by then the reality of blood-sucking ticks and the diseases they carried destroyed the romance of vampire films and literature. The woods had become my own Transylvania. The dogs and I were the hosts, the victims.

Ticks are hideous creatures, grotesquely unhuman, and lucky for us, they are so tiny we cannot see them with the unaided eye in their full monstrosity. Otherwise, we might never leave the safety of our homes. On the other hand, Dracula, although a monster in his own right, had human features, and because of this, I sympathized with him much of the time. Not so with ticks. With their eight legs, they look more like spiders; their mandibles under magnification make them look like crocodiles. When blown up with blood, their bodies swelling like balloons, ticks reach their most horrific blood-sucking form.

Although I might have hesitated before I drove the wooden stake through Count Dracula's heart, I have no problem torturing ticks. When I pull one off the dog and the woodstove is burning, I flip it in the firebox and wait for the satisfying pop of its bloody explosion. Feeling particularly malicious, I put a live tick on the red-hot burner of the kitchen stove and watch it dance to death before being incinerated into a few charred wisps. It's a childish vendetta.

Spiders, we know, have earned their own word for the fear they inspire—arachnophobia—but as far as I know, there is no word for fear of ticks. There should be, at least around here, since the chances of harm from a tick bite are a million times greater than those from a spider. Then again, we have no films or novels exploiting our fear of ticks. Maybe their harm is too real or new for popular art.

In William Hazlitt's essay "On the Pleasure of Hating," he watches a loathsome spider crawl across the room. Hazlitt does not lift his hand against the "unwelcome intruder." He resists "crushing the little reptile to death." He "bears the creature no ill-will, but still I hate the very sight of it." Hazlitt kept his "overt actions within the bounds of humanity. We give up the external demonstration, the *brute* violence, but cannot part with the essence or principle of hostility." I bear no ill will to spiders, to the daddy longlegs making their webs between the floor joists in the basement or up in the corners of our ceilings, for they do not carry a deadly bacteria or a virus, but toward ticks I demonstrate brute violence. My actions exceed the bounds of humanity, as I don't merely burn them or crush them to death. I actually take joy in demonstrating toward them as much hostility as possible.

I live and hunt in one of the most tick-infested regions of the United States—northern Wisconsin—home of the dreaded deer tick, *Ixodes scapularis*, carrier of much disease. In 2015 Wisconsin had a total of 3,267 cases of Lyme—1,300 confirmed, 583 probable, and another 1,384 estimated. Marathon County, where I reside, had 558 confirmed cases during the five years between 2007 and 2011, the highest number in the state. One of my favorite coverts, Transylvania, sits in the middle of the county, like a Lyme disease bull's-eye rash, surrounded by dozens of documented cases.

It's something to think about as I drive home from Transylvania, the driver's side window of my truck rolled down. As the ticks climb up my hunting pants, heading for the tender belly flesh between my belt and my shirt, I pick them off and pinch them between the fingernail of my thumb and index finger until I hear and feel a satisfying snap, the breaking of *I. scapularis*'s exoskeleton. Then I flip the dead tick out into the slipstream of clear October air. I do the same for the ticks crawling about the head and neck and back of whichever setter is next to me. On occasion, when the ticks are thick beyond belief, I banish the dog to the truck's box, and either Fergus or Jenkins, as the case may be, looks at me with a forlorn sadness through the sliding rear window of the cab. I feel sorry for them, but in the rearview mirror I can see ticks crawling about their white heads. They eventually resign themselves to their banishment, turn a few tight circles to make their bed, and settle in for the ride home. In extreme cases, I might stop on the way home for a tick cleansing. I grab the duct tape from a door's side pocket, smash writhing ticks to the sticky side, and when finished simply roll the tape up into a tight ball and throw it in the trash when I get home.

Once, on the way home from Transylvania, I picked over one hundred deer ticks off Ox's head. I can't remember how many I pulled off myself. At home, I picked another hundred off the dog for over two hundred total. Later, after returning from teaching an evening class, we picked even more ticks off Ox. We used up a lot of duct tape that day.

It all happened so quickly. I started to feel poorly at work on a Friday afternoon in early October—achy, feverish, the flu aura approaching—so I decided to head home. As I was pedaling up the last hill about a quarter of a mile from our house, my knees hurt so badly I almost had to get off my bike and walk. I got home and went straight to bed. By this time, I was shaking uncontrollably, so I piled on top of me all the blankets I could gather in my weakened state. I pulled on a stocking cap. The dogs jumped in bed with me, but even their heat did not lessen my chill. I was still shaking under the covers when Susan arrived home a few hours later. I had planned a full weekend of grouse hunting, but I never managed to get out of bed, let alone the house. The dogs moped around the house, their nails clicking on the wood floors as they paced about, wondering why we weren't out in the woods.

By Monday when I had to work, of course I felt somewhat better. I was able to get out of bed, but a nasty headache persisted. This went on for another week until I finally went to the doctor, Susan telling me I was a hard head for waiting so long. With a few rounds of antibiotics on board, I felt like myself again, the drugs acting with amazing swiftness, even though the pathogens continued to circulate in my bloodstream. This has also been our experience with the dogs we have treated for tick-borne illness—they bounce back within hours of treatment. We have had to pick them up to get them in the car to drive them to the vet. Administered antibiotics, they spring up from their beds and beg to go hunting the next day.

This easy recovery isn't always the case, however, and the long-term effects are frightening, as well as hard to diagnose. In the summer of 2016, at the age of eighty, Kris Kristofferson had to be relieved to find out he had *just* Lyme disease. Years earlier, after suffering several episodes of devastating memory loss, he had been misdiagnosed with Alzheimer's or some form of dementia stemming from the hard rock-and-roll living of his younger days. He was still sharp enough at times to begin writing a song about his descent into the dark, although he never got around to finishing the song.

In early 2016, a doctor on a hunch decided to test Kristofferson for Lyme disease, and the test came back positive. He must have felt like the ax had been lifted from his neck, not that Lyme disease is a picnic. It is, however, treatable, unlike Alzheimer's, and if caught early Lyme disease is reversible. In some cases, a course of antibiotics, usually doxycycline, knocks out the nasty spirochete, *Borrelia burgdorferi*, in a matter of days. One of our dogs with Lyme acted like he felt better about two hours after swallowing a marshmallow laced with a doxy pill.

Susan knows now that if I start exhibiting signs of dementia (Alzheimer's runs in my family) to first test me for Lyme disease. In case she is not around, I feel I should tape a piece of paper to my driver's license: IF I AM ACTING FORGETFUL, PLEASE TEST ME FOR LYME DISEASE.

I usually try to see the good in all things, especially nature, but that's difficult when it comes to ticks. Was I failing to see some hidden biological purpose they served? A friend who keeps guineas and chickens says they eat the ticks on his acreage, and he can't remember the last time he picked up a tick in his yard. Although I have never seen ticks in a ruffed grouse's crop, perhaps they, too, dine on them. Another friend says ticks keep the riffraff out of the woods, and they do keep people out of certain areas. I think twice about hunting a place like Transylvania. Other hunters must, too.

Last year I didn't hunt there until early December, after gun deer season and a couple of hard frosts. A dusting of snow had fallen overnight and covered the ground, the perfect amount of snow for seeing the tracks of whatever was moving around. We had a wonderful hunt, Fergus pointing a grouse in a balsam tree. The bird flushed from beneath the tree, like the perfect Christmas gift. We shot another bird about a hundred yards from that balsam. We flushed a total of a halfdozen birds that afternoon, which was a lot for that late in the season and the short amount of time we were in the woods. I figured either the bird numbers were high because they were so well fed on ticks or else the ticks had scared the riffraff out of the woods the entire season, eliminating the hunting pressure on the birds. *Maybe there was some good in ticks after all*, I thought, driving home.

Back home I had just dropped into my favorite chair next to the woodstove when I spotted two ticks scuttling up Fergus's forehead, heading for the soft tissue of his ears. He was already passed out on his dog bed next to the radiating warmth of the woodstove. *Really, snow on the ground, twenty degrees out, and these bastards yet live. Unbelievable.* I pulled them off his head, pinched them between my thumbnail and a fingernail, and dropped them onto the top of the woodstove. I waited a few seconds—*Pop! Pop!*—for those satisfying and bloody explosions. I bear much ill will toward these loathsome reptiles. I enjoy this brute violence.

EAST

Ackley

Losing Myself, Finding My Way

Ironically, we were saved by a cell-phone tower. I say that since I don't carry either a cell phone or GPS in the woods on my hunts. In fact, I rarely use a cell phone and have never used a handheld GPS device. At any rate, I don't know how we got turned around—other than I was just keeping up with the dog, moving through the woods, and not paying attention to landmarks. But eventually, after shooting and pocketing a grouse, I looked up and realized I had no idea where we were. Specifically, I mean. Generally, I knew we were north of the forty-fifth parallel, I knew the county we were in.

Susan could sense my bewilderment. "You don't know where we are, do you?" she asked. I gave her my standard answer: "Langlade County." We were standing with our setter in the midst of a claustrophobic aspen cutting. It's more like standing in a cornfield than in a forest, the trees pushing in, more than head high. None were tall enough to climb for a look-see. "It's that way," I said, nodding my head in the direction of where I thought we had parked the truck.

We started off in that direction, and the aspen slowly thinned and gave way, sloping down ever so slightly into tag alders, who love to stand with their roots in water. This wasn't a good sign, but I was determined to follow the compass due north, where we would eventually cut the state highway, which ran straight east/west for miles. Walk far enough, and we would sooner or later hit that concrete ribbon. The tag alders thinned, as I had feared, and gave way to marsh grass and an expansive swamp, the center of which was water. There was no sign of human activity across the swaying grass, cattails, and murky water. Not a road, not a trail, not a dike. No power lines, no barns, no silos. Nothing we could recognize. Terra incognito. Actually more like terror incognito.

Since it looked as if it was shorter to skirt around the swamp to the west, we took off in this direction, and I started to leave Susan behind. Fergus, oblivious to our anxiety, continued to hunt—business as usual for him, another new place to hunt. In fact, with his sense of smell he probably knew exactly where we were or in which direction to hike. Susan could sense the alarm in my rapid pace, my silence. I knew we could survive an October night in a northern Wisconsin swamp—the temperature wasn't supposed to drop below freezing— but I preferred my soft, warm bed to curling up with leaves and sticks.

Thoreau, in his essay "Walking, " wrote, "Hope and the future for me are not in lawns and cultivated fields, not in towns and cities, but in the impervious and quaking swamps." I understand Thoreau's faith and optimism in wildness, but at that moment, I would have liked nothing better than to saunter across a freshly clipped lawn and not grope across a quaking swamp. I was descending into hopelessness.

On the north side of this nameless marsh, the land tilted ever so slightly, a few feet at most, as evidenced by the larger trees growing in this drier soil: first more aspen, then balsam fir, white pine, a few hardy red oak. We continued north and once again the terrain sloped down and the maples and oaks thinned into aspen, which gave way to tag alders. It was just like before, and I had a panicky feeling we were moving in circles. When this passed and my reason returned, I told myself this could not be, because we had been faithfully following the red needle of my compass due north. *Maybe the compass was broken?*

I told my mind to shut up, and as the tags gave way once again to grass and we pushed into an opening, there was the cell tower, rising up into the low clouds above the flat landscape. This was a massive tower, at least several hundred feet tall, and I have no idea how we couldn't spot it earlier. It was on our left, to the west, and all along I had thought it would appear on our right, to the east. *Man, was I off.* Had my panic and fear hidden it in plain sight?

Seeing the tower, I felt all my fears drop into the rank, wet soil—we now had a landmark to lead us out to the highway and the towns and cities beyond. I took a bearing on the tower so even if trees obscured it, we could continue to track our way out and home. Our truck was parked another two hundred yards beyond the tall steel structure jutting into the sky. Even if it got dark, we could follow the blinking red lights in the blackest night.

We had to skirt yet another marsh, this time holding to the eastern shore, but eventually we did make it back to the truck, hunting more than three hours longer than we had planned. We shot only that single bird, having spent most of the time trying to find our way back to the truck and civilization, concentrating on getting out and home and not hunting.

No other outdoor activity gets me lost like grouse hunting. While cross-country skiing, we follow two tracks machine-groomed in the snow, or if we backcountry ski and break trail, we leave plain evidence of our passing. At any time, we can turn around and ski back in our tracks to where we started, unless the snow is drifting horribly and filling in the tracks. While hiking, mountain biking, or trail running, I follow a serpentine trail through the mountains, woods, or meadows, and these trails are typically well marked, often with maps at intersections: You Are Here. Just like the mall. I often hike logging roads and woods trails while hunting, but at some point on every hunt, the dog will pull me off trail and into the trackless woods. Other times, I call the dog and purposely go cross-country, avoiding the trails. Bushwhacking, that's what gets me turned around and disoriented.

Several times per year, I get deep enough in the woods in unfamiliar territory, look around, and wonder where I am. However, this is such a common occurrence for me I no longer panic as I did when it happened the first few times. This was years before GPS, which makes getting lost nearly impossible these days—if you carry it. Many do because we do not like to be lost, bewildered. I like that word, with wild or wilderness at its root, the landscape confusing us. We do not even like to be lost in the city, be-urbaned in the metroplex, which is why navigational systems are so popular in our vehicles. We're comforted by the notion: You Are Here.

Getting lost in the woods, however, just like getting lost in the city, is a time to discover and learn—about some new place in the world as well as about ourselves. Like Thoreau, we should regard it as a positive experience, not a negative one. "It is a surprising and memorable, as well as valuable, experience to be lost in the woods at any time," he wrote. Only by doing so would we "appreciate the vastness and strangeness of nature," and only when we are lost "do we begin to find ourselves, and realize where we are and the infinite extent of our relations."

I have found some of my favorite and most productive coverts while rambling around lost and bewildered. I have chanced across places of quiet beauty, tucked away in some far corner of the woods. In such a place, I wonder when the last human stopped here and rested. A few places striking me as unusual and worth revisiting I have never been able to find again. One was an old granite foundation, moss covered and crumbling on a high bank overlooking a creek. I know in general where it is, but I have never been able to stumble upon it again.

I have pioneered and learned to follow off-track routes through the woods, some tracings that I have used for years, connecting deer trails, old narrow-gauge railroad beds, rusting barbwire or stone fences, and waterways. I know which landmarks to use to take my bearings, following a towering white pine or turning slightly north in the crabapples past a pile of rocks that look like jumbled tombstones. Once while lost in a maze of logging roads—I had taken to snapping branches at intersections only to discover I was moving in circles— we stumbled across an astounding woodcock covert. By the end of the hunt, I had leashed the dog and heeled him at my side so he could no longer point. If I had let him point every woodcock, we wouldn't have made it out of the woods before dark. That covert still holds woodcock and the occasional grouse, although it was never as good as on that first day of bewilderment.

In the last century, our orienteering skills have deteriorated at alarming rates. We don't even know how to use paper maps much anymore. If nothing else, grouse and woodcock hunting is an exercise in finding our way through the woods, learning to see, read, and map the landscape. Rapid urbanization has exacerbated this loss. We learn to navigate the cityscape by reading traffic signs and road stripes, by memorizing billboards and buildings. With the imminent takeover of self-driving cars, we might completely forget how to use our minds and bodies to navigate through space. Let the machines do it.

Fear amplifies our reluctance to wander. Fear of the city, fear of the country, fear of the unknown lurking there. Most parents no longer let their children explore, in part because abductions are real, crime is real, and the children seem happy, or at least oblivious, plugged in in the backseat. As a kid growing up in a small Iowa town in the sixties and seventies, I had an insatiable desire to roam. Getting my first bicycle opened up an ever-widening world, the two wheels more efficient than my legs. I used my bicycle for both hunting and trapping expeditions. When I turned sixteen, I bought my first street-legal motorcycle, which increased my range tenfold. In all those years, I remember my parents being concerned about my safety only once and keeping me tethered close to home. The police had tracked an escaped convict to our area, flying helicopters and small airplanes over the cornfields in search of what we thought was most certainly a serial killer. I imagined his appearing at the end of one of the rows of the vast cornfield that ended a block from our house, materializing with foul intent and a bloody knife, intent on murdering our entire family like the killers in *In Cold Blood*. He was caught a county to the south and jailed, and my wandering resumed. Today, the innocence and freedom of that small-town life have, regrettably, all but disappeared from most places in this country.

Not only did I learn to make discoveries when lost as a kid, but I also learned to lose myself. Years later I have relearned this while grouse and woodcock hunting, and I lose myself mentally more often than physically, although both can happen simultaneously. One does not worry about the dirty dishes piled up next to the sink when trying to find a way out of the woods before dark.

Most of the time, while meandering along behind my dogs, I am thinking about something, usually whatever is consuming me at the time. In the best moments of grouse hunting, however, I lose the parts of myself not worth keeping. Like any enthralling experience, it consumes the trivial parts of our being. When the dog slows down and begins to make game, my predatory instincts kick in, and all of my senses focus on the immediate ground in front of us. My eyes and ears are on high alert; the dog's nose jumps into overdrive. I can see his nostrils flaring, his sides heaving, his head slowly turning as he deftly inserts his nose into a scent cone. Time alternately slows, stops, speeds up, jumps around, anything but running its normal, consistent pace.

During the chase, I find it impossible to fret about pressing bills or a leaking roof. I can't stew about an incompetent boss or suffer the agony of a jilted husband. The hunt crowds out all those thoughts. Fully engaged in the hunt, I don't even feel my physical ailments—the bunion on my right foot, the arthritis in my left shoulder, the Dupuytren's contracture in my trigger hand. The fatigue of the day even slides off my shoulders. It all falls away, in that one instant when the dog goes on point. It's as if I'm gone, or the only part of me left is the one sensing the nexus of bird, dog, shotgun, woods—the transcendent moment of grouse hunting.

I don't think my setters are ever physically lost. If they could write, they could function like GPS, smelling their way, and ours as well, out of the woods. Just as I can trace my ski tracks back home, they can follow our scent out of the woods. They know and follow the many secret scent paths in the woods, reading them like a map.

My setters also seem infinitely better at losing themselves, of focusing entirely on the world at hand at that moment. They can lose themselves chasing a leaf in the front yard. I wouldn't say dogs aren't self-conscious or they don't have doggy worries about a hard pad in their kennel or the neighbor's surly pit bull. If so, they don't obsess about these worries. When I pull on my hunting boots and grab my gun case, my dogs are gone for sure, lost to everything but the hunt. And in the best moments of a hunt, so am I.

The Fire Tower

It's the best view in the area, other than that from the observation tower on Rib Mountain, but that may not be saying much in the relatively flat Midwest. From up here on the ridge below the fire tower, I can see Rib Mountain thirty-some miles to the south, its single hump rising out of the landscape like a whale back breaching the ocean. If I had powerful enough binoculars, I could see the observation tower on top of the Rib, and I've often wondered, when I was up there, on which of the faraway ridges to the north did the old fire tower behind me perch.

I haven't made the pilgrimage up to the fire tower for over a decade. We discovered it shortly after we moved to the area, hiking the trail with a friend in the late summer. Susan and John climbed up to the top, leaving me and my acrophobia on the ground. Back then after a dry summer, it was manned, and the lookout invited them inside the cabin. They even got to use the fire finder, while I kicked around twigs and stones waiting for them to descend. Today, this lookout is no longer used.

To me, that day was the perfect fall day. In the morning, a hint of frost rimed the goldenrod and asters, which the sun quickly burnt off, and by noon the temperature had risen close to fifty. It felt a lot warmer, and I had stuffed my flannel shirt into my game bag before we were halfway up the climb to the tower. I tried to keep Fergus close because even in this cool weather he could overheat, but he is given to running big in the open woods, and these woods were mature and open, mostly maple and birch with some red oak and aspen mixed in. I had tied him to a lead and he was lying quietly next to me, panting lightly. He was not impressed with the view. Instead his nose twitched as he dissected aromas rising up out of the valley. He wanted to hunt, not sightsee, or sightsmell, as it may be.

The sky overhead was deep blue as only it can be in the clarity of October. I wondered if October Blue is a Crayola color. A few wispy clouds drifted overhead, some feathered like Fergus's tail, and I counted over a dozen contrails and wondered where the people were flying to and from as I sat back against an old birch in Flyover Country. It was hard to imagine Manhattan from up here.

The landscape rolling to the south looked as if it were on fire, a bright smokeless fire made with dry wood. The scarlet and golds of the maples almost hurt my eyes, testament that some of the best maple syrup country in the Midwest lay between here and Rib Mountain. The aspen and birch, both paper and yellow, were less impressive, their leaves drying into a creamy daffodil color, but they still caught my attention against the green of the conifers. I made a note of some of the aspen stands, particularly one that looked promising, and wondered how to get to it. I made a mental note to mark this aspen cutting on my hunting map under the driver's seat of my truck. Even as the woods were dying for the year, settling down and inward before the iron cold of winter, I wondered what drew me here, for the woods around the fire tower were open and mature, home to only an occasional grouse and then maybe just a bird on a crazy flight. I didn't even know if I should call this a covert or a hunt—it was more a nostalgic hike along a well-worn trail.

Hiking the trail up to the fire tower, I looked for a few pockets of clear-cut in these old woods, but the county foresters have left the trees, mostly sugar maple and red oak, to mature. If I had the time and inclination afterward, I could drive down the road after my fire tower hike and hunt a "real" spot, but that place would not have a view like this. In fact, most of my good spots to hunt grouse are downright claustrophobic. Some of them, the low and swampy ones, I hunt only on sunny days such as this, since they are too glum to enter on a sad, gray day. Our grouse woods in northern Wisconsin do not come with the sweeping views of Burton Spiller's or William Harnden Foster's New England or George Bird Evans's Appalachia. Nor do I hunt up in the rarefied air of eight thousand feet in the Rocky Mountains. Nevertheless, there is more than enough beauty for me here, enough small joys and surprises to keep me coming back. When I need a long view of the country, I hike up a hill like this to see this country roughed up by the last Ice Age ten thousand years ago.

In the early nineties when I was still discovering the country around here, I flushed a covey of at least ten grouse at the base of the climb up to the fire tower. At the time, I didn't know there was a tower up on the ridge, but I kept following the trail deeper into the woods and climbing higher up the ridges, my eyes still wide from that stunning covey flush. I hadn't shot at a single one as the dog waded into a tangle of sumac and blackberry and the birds flushed as one, like a covey of quail. I don't even think I flicked the safety off my old Valmet. I keep hoping for a flush like this, for a return to the good old days of the late nineties when birds were so plentiful they seemed to pop out from beneath the stones.

Fergus got up and stretched, bowing to the south in a downward-facing dog, and squeaked out a yawn. He looked at me with ears back and wags a low tail slowly—his beggar look. It was time to be going. *Please*, his eyes seemed to plead.

When I was younger and influenced much more by an itchy trigger finger, I came here looking for birds. In time and with more grouse experience, I learned that this cover, even though beautiful, simply was never going to hold many birds unless the county started to cut more trees and the younger growth that grouse and woodcock depend on replaced the mature maples and oaks. I didn't want to waste my time here once I figured that out. I hunted only where I could reliably find birds, scenery be damned.

But these days I'm looking for more than just birds. Killing isn't as important to me as it once was. My predatory drive still glows inside me, but it's now a banked fire and not a raging inferno. Perhaps I have low testosterone and need a pill, but that would imply the way I feel about hunting and how I practice it today isn't quite what it should be, as if a bulging game bag is the only way to hunt.

There are other ways to hunt, though, like what I call "counting coup." I call it this even though Native Americans practiced this on their enemies, getting close enough to touch them without killing them. For one, I don't consider grouse and woodcock to be my enemies, nor are we warring against each other. I'm the only one with the dog and the shotgun, and only the grouse or woodcock has something, everything actually, to lose. These birds have only their wings and wit with which to escape.

I don't have enough skill to get close enough to reach out and touch a grouse or a woodcock, unless the woodcock is less than a couple of weeks old. My counting coup, if I can call it that, is flushing a pointed bird and watching it fly away without shooting—the act with all save the killing, a sort of shoot and release. At most, I might track the bird with my shotgun as it flutters through the treetops and yell, "*Bang!*" You would think this would bother my dogs, since I wasn't holding up my end of the bargain, but neither Fergus nor Jenkins seems to mind, and they course after the next bird with just as much enthusiasm. For sure, *they* don't need a shot of testosterone to jolt their predatory instincts. Imagine what a cup of coffee would do for them.

I practice shoot and release on woodcock much more than I do on grouse. I have often wondered why I have this bias. Some hardcore grouse hunters refuse to hunt woodcock and look upon them with disdain, as if they were child's play. I get the same sort of feeling from deer hunters who shoot only bucks. I've seen the looks from grizzled veterans when I bring a nice fat doe into the registration station. They throw their scorn in my direction for violating their unwritten code: a doe, any kid can shoot one of those. Like a mature buck, ruffed grouse are much more of a challenge to hunt than woodcock, especially with a pointing dog. They are the more skittish bird and don't hold well for the dog, as woodcock typically do. It follows in my thinking that the greater the challenge the greater the reward, and so I have placed grouse higher than woodcock in my prey hierarchy, but I do enjoy woodcock hunting and make a point of being out there specifically to hunt woodcock on their opening day, usually a week later than the grouse opener in Wisconsin.

While banding woodcock in the spring, I've handled day-old woodcock chicks, cute little clowns with their oversized feet. The intimate contact, holding a fuzzy little yellow ball so innocent—well, how could anyone shoot one of these creatures? Even the adults seem more innocent than ruffed grouse, sitting there relying on their camouflage sometimes inches from the dog's nose. That rarely happens with a grouse, although on occasion a young bird will flush up into a tree and look down on you with much the same innocence. Shooting that bird out of the tree, to me, seems about as appropriate as blasting a woodcock chick. I suppose what I'm trying to say is I want to give the quarry a fair and sporting chance, although I don't think a woodcock or a grouse much cares about how it is killed. It just wants to keep on living, so this philosophical question matters only to the hunter. My setters don't engage in such philosophical gymnastics—they simply and without question want to hunt.

Maybe it's the woodcock's large eyes. We know from research that humans feel more empathy toward animals that look like us and have our same features. This is why we can rip the wings off a fly or torch ants with a magnifying glass; however, we would never even think of trying to chop off the legs of our dog. Woodcock have those large dark eyes, and if you have ever received one from the dog with its head up staring you down . . . I have a much more difficult time dispatching woodcock than I do grouse. I blame the woodcock's eyes.

Aldo Leopold wrote that once he understood the woodcock's biology, he could no longer think of the bird as just a feathery target: "No one would rather hunt woodcock in October than I, but since learning of the sky dance I find myself calling one or two birds enough. I must be sure that, come April, there will be no dearth of dancers in the sunset sky." You could argue the ruffed grouse has an equally interesting mating history, and I can't imagine the woods in spring without the sound of drumming grouse—the *put, put, put* into the quick drumlike roll—on its log. Knowing the grouse drums on a log doesn't make me less inclined to shoot them.

Population surveys show that woodcock numbers are declining, due mostly to habitat loss. In my lifetime, I have seen bag limits drop from five to three, and the season shortened from sixty to forty-five days in response to this serious decline. Not shooting as many wood-cock seems a way of preserving them, missing them as an act of con-servation. But since I know of the ruffed grouse's infamous cycle, I don't feel as if my predation has an effect on the population. The birds will cycle up and down every ten or so years, and my efforts will not stop this periodic booming and busting. Counterintuitive as it is, research suggests that human predation little affects overall popula-tion levels. In the end, it seems I feel more pity for woodcock and less for ruffed grouse, which probably makes little sense, unless you have held dying birds of both species in your hands.

I was thinking about my ruffed grouse bias as we hiked down from the tower and out of the woods, and was startled to find that we were almost back to the truck. I had let Fergus roam out a little too far and so I stopped and whistled for him. He was a hundred yards ahead of me down in a wet depression off the trail. "Fergus, *come!*" I yelled. He looked up and started to make his way back to me. I took a step and the ground exploded at my feet. A grouse thundered up—a sound I dream—and flew directly down the trail. Instinctively my hands clutched the air looking for a shotgun, but it was slung across my shoulders. My hands were empty. The instinct to shoot at that sound is etched in my brain and hardwired into my eyes, arms, and hands.

I didn't need a pill after all—I was still very much a predator.

Lake Ament

Body Count Grouse

Fergus bounded up into the truck's bed after a bit of coaxing and plopped down on the dirty old remnant of carpet there, muzzle between his paws. He was heat beat. I pulled a bird out of my vest, smoothed back the breast feathers, and tried to coax the tail back into a distinctive ruffed grouse fan. Then I pulled out two more and arranged all three birds on the tailgate, placing the one brown phase grouse between the two grays, and artistically positioned my tattered Filson vest, my shotgun, and a few spent shells alongside Fergus, who was looking on with drooping eyes. With the tableau arranged, I took several pictures, maybe a dozen, then rearranged the birds, teased out the fans again, and shot probably a dozen more from different angles. I had to make squeaky noises to get Fergus's attention and get him to look at the camera, but finally, after scrolling through the shots, I was fairly confident I had at least one good one.

By most accounts, we had had a very successful day. It was still the first week of the season, mid-September, and the heavy feel of summer still hung in the air. We had left the house early, just after sunup, because I knew Fergus, with his heat intolerance, would be done for the day by ten o'clock, maybe sooner. I was sure that by then he would flop on the ground with his tongue lolling out of his mouth,

A dog-tired Fergus in a tailgate pose. (Mark Parman)

acting as if he were hyperventilating, a sure sign he was overheating. He has run himself into rhabdomyolysis, running so hard his muscle tissue breaks down and dumps into his bloodstream. He, regrettably, does not have a governor that measures out his pace. A heavy dew overnight had wet me to the waist, but the moisture did little to help to cool Fergus.

We started the morning in a covert I call Lake Ament, which we would hunt first, followed by a smaller covert a half mile or so down the road from Lake Ament; each would take less than an hour to hunt. We would be back home well before noon. By then, the temperature was predicted to be near seventy, and both of us would be napping, college football on the TV.

In the first covert, we put up seven birds in head-high popple, less than two hundred yards down the trail. They were young-of-the-year birds, coveyed up. I had just finished shoving shells into my gun when Fergus started to make game and in short order went on point. According to my journal, four birds flushed initially, followed by three more. On the initial flurry, I missed a bird with the first barrel and hit one with the second. Luckily, and I do mean that, I had time to reload before the final three flushed, and I dropped one bird from that group.

We collected the birds, and it was easy to tell from their three-quarter-sized bodies and smaller fans they were young of the year. As I slid them into my game bag, I felt a twinge of remorse for slaughtering birds who had lived only a few months. When the birds coveyed up again after we moved on, would they notice two of their members were missing? Even so, those young birds were a sign of an increasing population. We were moving toward the peak of the grouse cycle.

Before finishing the loop through the covert, I had missed two more singles, the shooting difficult as I tracked them through the verdant green, a wall of vegetation. As we drove down the road to the next patch of woods, I made a mental note to return and hunt here later in the season when the leaves had fallen.

Our luck continued in the next aspen cutting. Fergus pointed three birds, and I shot at two and bagged one, this one a large, mature bird. This grouse made the other two look like the children they were. In about an hour of hunting, we had collected three birds, what I called the Iowa limit, a marker where I often call it quits. By law, we could shoot two more grouse, but I was more than satisfied by the way the day had turned out. Besides, it was getting warm. A one-bird total for the day would have made me happy—and I told myself I needed to photograph them to record our accomplishment so we could remember this humid September day. *We were quite the hunters, Fergus and I.*

On the drive back to Wausau, I took the long way home to look at some more coverts I intended to hunt later in the season as well as to stop at the convenience store in Gleason. There, I bought us each a reward for our triumph—a refill of coffee for me and a beef stick for Fergus, who wolfed the dry meat down in two bites like it was a marshmallow.

Later that evening, after my nap, I downloaded the pictures onto my computer, selected the best one, and posted it to Facebook: the tailgate shot, the victims spread out in a body count for all to see, the picture of hunting success. I have saved many such pictures, shots of all my dogs next to lifeless birds that go back several years. I have similar pictures of me from the eighties, posing in front of dead Iowa pheasants.

What I don't have are pictures of all the days we came home emptyhanded, yet equally, if not more, successful. Or the days of total failure, like the day last year when Fergus bumped at least a dozen woodcock in a row, maybe more—in frustration I stopped counting all his mistakes. He walked right over them as if they weren't there and he didn't smell them. After the first couple of bumps, I scolded him, just mildly irritated, and by the third and fourth, I whoa-ed him and set him up, kicking the brush around in front of his nose and telling him to be careful. By the tenth bump, Susan was starting to worry about my blood pressure. I have no explanation for his erratic behavior. He hasn't done this since; he hadn't done it before. Needless to say, I did no Facebook posting that evening, and Fergus spent the evening dug deep into his kennel, pouting about the tongue lashing he had received, or maybe he just didn't want to be around me.

After reading research about the effects of Facebook and other social media (often from the sources of my students' research papers), I've revised my thoughts about the tailgate shot and what constitutes a successful hunt. Essentially, the research shows, our self-presentation on Facebook gives our friends out in cyberland a distorted view of who we are. We record only the highs of our lives and not the lows. We present ourselves in the best possible light—*look at me, I never miss and my dog points every grouse he encounters.* In defense of the tailgate shot, it's a cliché, a behavior we find ourselves falling into; plus, it's meaningless to photograph nonexistent birds. An empty game bag doesn't make for an exciting shot, although it can sometimes tell a great story.

Americans are enthralled by numbers. We think the best jobs are those paying the most, or the best quarterback is the one throwing for the most yards. The best wine costs the most; the best grouse or woodcock hunter shoots the most birds, day in, day out. It is a black-and-white means of comparison, a simple way to compare ourselves with others and define our success or lack thereof.

But ultimately, the tailgate shot misses most of the story: the dog work (hard to photograph), the miles walked, the way the tops of the aspen etch their highest branches into the blue of an October sky, or the sweet autumnal-rot smell of the woods during bird season. So perhaps I should start photographing empty tailgates to chronicle all those good days, all those other good things happening moment by moment on each hunt.

Left Lot Covert

Reflections of a Left-Handed Shooter

Growing up, I idolized Cincinnati Reds and Hall of Fame catcher Johnny Bench, so naturally I wanted to be a catcher like him. Besides, it was the toughest and most involved position on the diamond. There was one problem, however: I was left-handed, and lefties simply did not play catcher. Doing so back then was like growing your hair over your ears or not wearing a belt.

I kept bugging the coach to just let me try to play catcher, just give me one chance at it, but the coach said we didn't have a mitt for me and I couldn't catch with a fielder's glove. My father, in all other things a staunch conservative who never questioned tradition or routine, went out and bought me a crisp new Rawlings left-handed catcher's mitt, and ultimately I got to catch on our high school baseball team. I am still so fond of that mitt, thirty-five years later I occasionally use it in a backyard game of catch.

My father, however, wasn't as knowledgeable or concerned when it came to hunting and shotguns. For my first shotgun, my father handed me a bolt-action Mossberg .410, a gun good for squirrels, possibly rabbits, definitely not the pheasants I dreamed of shooting over Iowa sloughs. The Mossberg's right-handed bolt and right-handed safety were simply too awkward for me. The first time I fired that gun at a rooster, I missed point blank with the first shot and jammed the second shell trying to jack it in the breech. By the time I ejected the first casing and got another shell in the chamber, that bird was a speck on the horizon.

Left-handers reportedly comprise about a tenth of the world's population, a percentage the experts tell us has remained constant throughout history. Researchers have yet to figure out why some people insist on using their left hand as the dominant one. Yet walk into a gun shop and scan the racks. Significantly less than 10 percent of the guns are left-handed. You might be lucky to find one in a hundred, and in most instances, a left-handed gun buyer will need to special-order a gun to fit his or her inclination.

After missing that pheasant, I decided to teach myself to be a switch-shooter—after all, I had taught myself how to switch-hit. I would shoot the Mossberg right-handed as it was designed to be shot. For some reason, however, I was never able to get the hang of switch-shooting as I did switch-hitting. When I shouldered it right-handed, my dominant left eye always pulled my head to the right to sight down the barrel, and the position of my arms, shoulders, and neck never felt right. I went back to shooting it from the left, figuring I would at least get in one good shot if I could slip the safety off, and maybe that single shot would teach me focus and concentration. Years later, when my nephew discovered the old Mossberg gathering cobwebs in my parents' basement, he asked if he could borrow it. "Sure," I said, "it's yours. Keep it." He acted as if he had just won the lottery. He had no idea I was thinking good riddance. I had never hit a bird in flight with that gun.

As a young man, I carried another shotgun, a Remington 870 lent to me by my future in-laws—perhaps as an early test of my ability to compromise. It was a right-handed model, of course. I carried that pump gun upside down with my left thumb on the safety, an awkward way to carry a gun, but the only way I could reliably flick off the safety when a rooster exploded out of the grass in my vicinity. It was a 12 gauge, though, a significant improvement in firepower over the .410. I nearly shot myself in the foot with that gun when I tripped walking a brushy terrace and my thumb slipped off the safety and my finger in the trigger guard pulled the trigger. The blast tore a hole in the earth several yards in front of my toes, and I never carried that gun again. Years later, I was amazed to learn that Remington made the 870 in a left-handed model, when I stopped by a friend's cabin and he had one hanging by the sling near the front door. My friend was also a notorious dyslexic, a condition much more prevalent with lefties.

We hear dozens of myths and sayings about lefties, such as their being more creative or not living as long as right-handed people, neither notion proven true. Many cultures have folk tales of lefties being of the devil, practicing black magic, going down Satan's path (on the left), and even our own political left has a tinge of the deviant in many contexts. Jesus sits on the right-hand side of God; judgment strikes from the left-hand side.

In German, "right" (*recht*) means correct or legal, while "left" (*links*) connotes something underhanded or questionable and *linkisch* means clumsy. "Sinister" comes from the root word of *sinestra*, which means left-handed in Latin. Many languages have sayings that, roughly translated, mean to do something with two left hands, that is, poorly or unskillfully. No wonder I'm such a poor shot—I'm shooting from the left, or the devil's side. The wrong side.

But really, what am I to do, given that I'm left-eyed? In fact, research suggests many more shooters are left-eye dominant than the 10 percent of the population that is left-handed. My wife, for instance, is left-eye dominant, yet shoots right-handed. She tried switching to the other side, as I did as a kid, but doing so felt awkward and soon she was back to the right side and trying to close her left eye when shooting so the right would take over. Other left-eyed shooters who shoot from the right side put a small dot of tape on the left lens of their shooting glasses to block the dominant left eye, forcing themselves to use the right. It's a serious handicap for a shooter, particularly in the field where shots are sporadic and unpredictable.

I own half a dozen shotguns, and only one of them is specifically a left-handed gun, a 12 gauge Benelli Montefeltro. I have three over-and-unders, including a pair of Browning Superlight Feathers, guns that are ambidextrous, a word that, by the way, exhibits right-handed bias. It uses the Latin root word *dexter* (right) and means literally "right-handed" (skillful) on both sides. You read earlier what having two left hands means—maladroit, inept, graceless. I also shoot a 20 gauge Ithaca 37 Ultra Featherlight, a pump gun that bottom loads and ejects, another ambidextrous gun.

Sometimes I like to slide the pump back and forth on this gun, just to hear the clean clacking of the action and to feel the thunk of the bolt snapping into place through the walnut of the stock and forearm piece. This shotgun feels good in my hands—my fingers curled around the walnut, the heft of a just-right tool—but this is something I don't readily admit these days. Many people are afraid of guns and tremble at the thought of seeing or, worse, actually holding one. They would drop one with a shriek, as if it was a snake or a bat if one ever found its way into their hands. In short, to many people guns are simply anathema. But my chainsaw scares me much more than any of my shotguns or rifles, in part because it was designed for a righty, built backward for me. Unlike a lightweight bird gun, the chainsaw in my hands feels like an angry tomcat, snarling and jumping, always ready to lash out and slice me if I let down my guard. A few people think we shouldn't be killing birds or cutting trees and both tools are obsolete, or should be made so, in today's world.

You would think I would lavish special care on my Benelli—my only left-handed gun—but I have abused it. Twice I have driven off with this gun on the top of my truck. The second time I did so, I pulled away from Left Lot Covert, drove ten miles down a state highway, through two ninety-degree corners at sixty miles per hour, and on into a convenience store in Merrill, where my shotgun slid off the topper and smashed into the asphalt parking lot. I was completely ignorant of this as I happily perused the aisles of the convenience store, basking in the glow of a successful hunt, until a woman shopper stuck the gun in my face, arm extended, as if it was a full diaper she really didn't want to touch. "Is this yours?" she asked. "I think it fell off the top of your truck."

Instead of grabbing the gun, I bolted out to my truck to confirm what deep down I knew I had done. Behind the seat, unzipped and empty, sat the case. I rushed back into the store and claimed my now sadly wrecked shotgun. The barrel was canted ten degrees or so off center (some serious cast on), and the stock was cracked behind the trigger guard. The barrel was scraped, the front sighting bead broken off. It was in sad shape.

It's not normal to be standing in a convenience store with a 12 gauge, not even in a gun-crazy place like northern Wisconsin, especially when a deputy sheriff is in the store. He marched over and I was expecting to get tased or cuffed, or at the very least receive a citation or a harsh reprimand. Afterward, I was surprised he didn't draw his pistol and scream at me to slowly place the gun on the floor and back away. Instead, he grabbed the shotgun and said, "Hey, isn't that a lefty?" Then he swung it around the store—left-handed and deftly, I might add—at imaginary targets: the sign for specials on hotdogs (two for three dollars) and the Leinenkugel's beer ad over the door. "What is this?" he asked, peering at the action. "A Benelli, sir," I answered. He threw it up to his shoulder again and practiced his swing a few more times before handing it back to me. "Nice gun. You should take better care of it," he said as I took my battered gun. "Yes, sir." The gun I should love the most, I abuse.

Being left-handed isn't always a disadvantage. Sure, there is the problem of eating at a crowded table and bumping elbows with righties, or the problem of spiral-bound notebooks and guitars. A left-handed shooter, though, can use the abnormality to advantage, just as a left-handed boxer, batter, or fencer can do so since the competition thinks mainly from the right. Ninety percent of the competition comes at them from the right side, the usual side, and a lefty can exploit this.

When shooting a shotgun, a lefty swings more naturally from left to right, just as a righty swings more naturally from right to left. Because of this, I like to line up on the right side when hunting in a group and walking in on a point, since the birds crossing out my side typically flush into my strength. When I walk in on the dog's point, I always try to do so from the right side. If I'm with a partner, I line him on the left side of the dog, a problem for my brother, who is left-handed as well. (I don't know if he has figured out my ploy after all these years hunting together.) My wife and I form a natural team since she is right-handed and shoots better at birds crossing her left side.

Last November, we returned to Iowa to hunt pheasants for the first time in many years, staying and hunting with Susan's family in southwestern Iowa. It was marginal hunting until our last day, when a cold front roared down from Canada, dropping a skift of snow and ushering in an icy northwestern wind. There were six of us out that day, plus two dogs. As we started out, Susan's sister, Cindy, in charge of wangling the bunch, asked which side of the ditch I wanted to work. "Right," I said immediately. On the right side, Fergus would be working nose into the wind, and on a hunch, I figured the birds would get up and take to the wind, flushing left to right, using the arctic tailwind to aid their escape.

Fergus, who had worked only ruffed grouse and woodcock in his seven years of bird hunting, had yet to figure out what we were doing in Iowa. He thought the picked cornfields were barren and kept lighting out for whatever trees were on the horizon. (A confirmed grouse and woodcock dog, maybe he was exhibiting a version of left-handedness.) Maybe it was the wind direction, maybe the trees were too far off to entice him. I have no idea how he learned to point a pheasant, but that day everything clicked for him. The roosters were holding tight under the snow-covered grass, and they were coming up big and slow as zeppelins before they caught the wind and tore off to the southeast.

At first, I thought I had blown it when the initial rooster flushed, and I missed with both top and bottom barrel. Fergus had locked up and I was kicking around in some head-high turkey-foot grass in front of him, thinking it was a close sitting hen if anything. Then six hens and a cackling rooster burst out of the snow and withered grass and almost knocked me down. The multiple flush stunned me, but I should have carefully picked the rooster out of the hens and dropped him. Oh, the disappointment. I could endure the scorn and taunts of my in-laws on the other side of the ditch, but I could have slapped myself for having blown Fergus's first point.

I needn't have worried because Fergus wasn't fazed, and he was shortly on point again. I walked in on the right side of Fergus, kicking up a nice rooster burrowed into the grass. I had to shoot quickly before it got going up in the tailwind, but grouse hunting is a great teacher for quick shooting. Three more birds got up into the wind and flushed left to right, and we soon collected four roosters.

Before we had reached the turnaround at a rusty barbwire fence on which hung a No Trespassing tire, I had broken open my shotgun and was working the dog for Susan and Cindy and watching the sisters hunt. The weight of those birds cut into my shoulders on the trek back to the truck, but the burden was pleasant, and I was warm knowing that whatever would come, we would always have this blustery day under a hard blue Iowa sky with Fergus on point in the snow. He had finally figured out how to point and hold a pheasant.

As we were sitting on the tailgate, Cindy asked me how I knew the birds would flush our way. "I didn't. I just wanted to work Fergus into the wind," I said. I didn't want to tell her the whole story—of how I had set myself up for the easiest shots possible for a lefty. That was a bit devilish, an old left-hander's trick.

Old Man Covert

It's a good thing nasty washboards riddled the gravel road as it wound through the county forest because they slowed me down through the corners as the truck skittered diagonally across them. For balance, Jenkins leaned into the corner and dug his toenails into the passenger seat where he was sitting upright as my copilot. As we exited one of the final corners and approached the paved county highway, a white, four-legged form zipped across the road in front of us and plunged into the woods of the opposite ditch. Jenkins stood up and barked at the movement as it dove into the brush. I thought, *That looked like a setter.*

I skidded to a stop, then backed up to where the dog had disappeared, thinking he might shoot out of the woods again, but no dog materialized despite Jenkins's frantic barking. After a few minutes I pulled away and rolled cautiously down the road, tires crunching gravel. Around the next corner we came upon a bent figure shuffling our way. He was wearing a blaze hat and carrying a semiautomatic shotgun. He stopped when he saw us approaching, and I rolled down the window as I pulled up to a stop next to him. His face was creased, his hair all gone white where it hung below his cap. He walked like my grandfather who had farmed for sixty years walked—stiff, stooped a bit, like his joints needed oiling. "How's it going?" I asked. "Not too bad," he answered in a strong southern drawl.

"You're not from around here, I take it," I said jokingly, and he laughed. "Nice dog you got there," he said. Jenkins was standing in the seat and banging his tail against the dash and the seat. "I always did like tricolors."

In a few moments, we were joined by another hunter, who popped out of the woods on our left. This was the old man's son, I learned shortly. The old man was eighty-three and had always wanted to hunt grouse and woodcock in the Northwoods. "And I'm not getting any younger, so here we are." Soon their setter, Dixie, joined us. I hadn't been seeing things after all.

It wasn't a long conversation and was mostly small talk, but before I rolled up the window and drove on, I suggested they drive down the road a bit to the north and take the third logging road to the right. Follow that east a couple of hundred yards to the blue rocks blocking the road — graffiti rocks for the local teenagers — and hunt the faint old logging road directly south of the rocks. "You can't miss the popple cutting." They thanked me, and we drove off for home.

I'm not one to give out my coverts, especially to out-of-state strangers, but this time was different. I wanted to help the old man get some birds, just as I would want someone to do the same for me if I'm ever in that shape and situation. I also didn't want to see their setter squashed on the moderately busy gravel road they were hunting. ATVs routinely raced up and down it, going forty to sixty miles an hour, recklessly joyriding. I had driven up and down that road for twenty-five years and never had thought once of hunting it, thoroughfare through the county forest that it is. And lest you think me a saint, the spot I had offered up was really just a good woodcock covert. It held only the occasional grouse. I am downright stingy with grouse coverts. The faint old logging trail, although not as smooth as the well-trafficked gravel road they were on, would make for easy walking for the old man, and with any luck he would get a shot at a woodcock or two.

I knew there were woodcock by the blue rocks because we had just been through there to finish our hunt and put up half a dozen. In fact, Jenkins did something I will never forget. Since I don't put beeper collars on my dogs (a practice I'm starting to rethink), I lost him in the dense popple. This was early October and the leaves were still fast on most of the trees. After a few minutes, I hollered for him. He was maybe thirty yards away, below me on a hillside, hard on point. He left the point and took a few steps toward me, and I heard the faint clank of his bell. When we made eye contact, he crept back to where he was and locked back into the point he had left. I literally starting laughing, not really sure that what I had seen had just happened. I walked in on the point past Jenkins, flushed the bird, and watched it fly away. Jenkins did this same feat once again later in the year, and I had to laugh again. It wasn't textbook pointing technique on his part, but oh for a video camera in that situation.

I do hope the old man and his son from Tennessee got a crack at a few woodcock.

After I wrote *A Grouse Hunter's Almanac*, I received a half-dozen letters from readers. Real letters in envelopes, with stamps and postmarks, delivered by the US Postal Service. Two of the writers were over ninety. One gentleman from out east was ninety-two and said he had to give up hunting along with his dog a few years previous. The return address was an apartment in a place called Sunset Ridge or Happy Acres, clearly a retirement villa of sorts. Not knowing what to say, I sent him back a short thank-you note and wished him well. At first his story depressed me, but then the more I thought about his age, I realized he had truly been blessed if he could still hunt at ninety. I marvel that George Bird Evans was still going strong at ninety and can only hope for that kind of longevity. For sure, I will feel grateful if I make it that far and am still hunting. I know other hunters who give it up at seventy or seventy-five.

Grouse and woodcock hunters, like hunters in general, are a dying breed, a trend alarming to departments of natural resources and wildlife groups, such as the Ruffed Grouse Society. Their funding is directly tied to license sales and memberships, and so they are trying to recruit younger members as well as women, an effort that I laud, but those coming into the fold are not keeping up with those leaving it.

There are many causes for this decline in grouse and woodcock hunters. Some experts cite video games and the internet, our young people's fascination with screens and technology. For many kids, it's much more interesting and engaging to play World of Warcraft than hunt. Others blame the efforts of animal rights groups to smear hunters and note our changing, urbanized values, or, as I heard a hunter once say, "the metrosexualizing of the USA." He spit after he growled this, to punctuate his contempt. Then there's the curmudgeon complaining about kids being too soft these days and wanting everything handed to them by their helicopter parents, usually voiced by the guy who said he walked five miles to school in a June blizzard.

Urbanization, to me, seems the crucial factor: the loss of connection to a wild landscape and a place to hunt. Americans in the last fifty years have left the country and small towns in droves, moving to the city and its suburbs. Consequently, many hunters today don't have a place to hunt or it's too far away for consistent access. Growing up, I walked one block east, slipped over a barbwire fence, and started hunting a cornfield. I could do this after school if I hustled home, even in the short afternoons of late autumn. Today, 90 percent of Americans live in cities or suburbs, with limited access to wildlife areas and populations. This is nobody's fault—it just is.

Demographics are changing rapidly in America as well. Let's face it—we grouse and woodcock hunters are mostly white and male, and getting older with each passing season. One of the most sobering reminders of this is the "In Memoriam" column for members of the Loyal Order of Dedicated Grouse Hunters in Ken Szabo's newsletter, *Grouse Tales*. In each issue, we can read of two or three members who have crossed over into Tinkhamtown. We are a dying breed, and if we expect our sporting tradition to remain viable, we should be encouraging all people to take up the sport, including women and minorities, especially the kids.

I don't picture myself as some last hunter in the woods. It's not as if I have the woods to myself. Somedays I drive to a favorite covert, and there's a truck or two parked there, dog kennels in the back. On those days I think there are too many grouse hunters. Statistically, though, I'm in a dwindling minority.

For thousands of years, humans hunted and gathered, but now we drive to the grocery store and very few people think this odd. It's as if we had been doing this for our entire history. Hunting, killing your own food, is looked at today as the anomaly, as abnormal human behavior. A cartful of Doritos, hotdogs, and diet Mountain Dew—that's the norm.

Whatever the causes and effects of the changing social landscape on hunting, I mostly think about it in the context of what it's like for me to grow old as a grouse hunter. I'm in my midfifties and have hunted grouse for about twenty-five years. I like to think I'm at the peak of my upland career—twenty-five years going up and twenty-five years dropping back down, if I'm lucky. I don't believe the old saw about the latter half all downhill. At a certain age, grouse hunting gets hard physically, and although wisdom and experience can compensate for some of the decline, it doesn't replace a young pair of legs, lightning reflexes, keen ears, and sharp eyesight.

I recently bumped into an eighty-year-old hunter in the Fleet Farm parking lot who was watering an ancient and rickety-looking setter. I pulled in, jumped out, and introduced myself to both the hunter and the dog. We talked for some time as I scratched his old dog behind the ears. When I got home, Susan asked, "Where have you been, honey?" I had been gone almost two hours shopping for dog food. The old hunter said he had a place up north but didn't go there much anymore. One hunting companion had died, another had dementia, and a third had moved out West. For those who thrive on the camaraderie of the hunt, losing friends would color October dark. I imagine it's much like losing a beloved dog, maybe worse.

As a young hunter, I never once questioned whether I had the stamina to hunt all day. In fact, I longed for the day when I could retire, so I could hunt all day, every day. Hunt all day every day for ninety days—what a dream. I had heard old people complain about arthritis, bunions, cardiac problems, a bum knee, but with a healthy body I really didn't get it. I had seen friends and family grow old and decrepit, watched as my father wasted away from Alzheimer's, but I didn't really understand the experience of aging until it showed up on my doorstep. I didn't have the language for it, the terms to contemplate the process, the wear and tear, which normally occurs to a human body. Like cars or dishwashers, we wear out and break down. It's only when we see an old model in exceptional shape that we take note—did you see that old Ford F-150? It didn't have a spot of rust on it.

My father's struggle with Alzheimer's brought home my own frailty and mortality, as did the day when I felt a stabbing pain in the left side of my chest and wondered if I was having a heart attack. I was close to an hour from my parking spot; I hadn't left a note on the kitchen counter telling Susan where I was hunting; I didn't own a cell phone, not that it would have worked where I was. *How would my setter get out of the woods if I crumped here?* Later, a checkup with my doctor revealed a condition called costochondritis, an inflammation of the cartilage connecting ribs to breastbone, which I've since learned is aggravated by carrying a shotgun around the woods. On long hunts of more than two hours, I often thread a sling on my old Ithaca M37. The sling gets hung up on the brush, and a few of my friends who fancy side-by-sides scoff at my pump gun. It isn't a classic grouse gun, and I often forget to pump it for a second shot, but it sure helps ease the pain. And I'm not fooled into thinking I'm having cardiac arrest way out in the backwoods.

I don't know what to think of my cooling lust to kill. As a young man, I wanted to drop every bird that got up in front of me. I replayed missed shots and the dogs screwing up points over and over in my head ad nauseam. I wailed and gnashed my teeth when this happened. Today, a game bag full of birds isn't as important, although a day when I shoot two or three birds is still special. What's changed is that I can call one bird or even no birds a successful hunt. I don't force myself out of the house in a downpour or a howling wind, both of which wreak havoc on the dog work and make a hunter miserable. I don't care how expensive your raingear is, sooner or later, you will be soaked to the skin, wandering around a dripping woods. I suppose I should have my testosterone checked.

There are benefits to aging. I now have more time and money as retirement looms around the corner. I foresee a day when I can hunt Monday through Friday and take the weekends off when the woods are fuller, or simply hunt when the weather is good. I don't have to worry about where the money will come from if I need a case of shells or a new pair of boots. When I first started grouse hunting in my twenties, I traded away my old single shot on my first over-and-under because I needed the fifty bucks from the single to go toward the double. I felt guilty for weeks about buying such a fancy gun. I haven't shot it for years, as I've graduated to lighter shotguns, and it mostly gathers dust. Within reason, I can buy any shotgun that takes my fancy, which these days means a light gun.

Time seems to flow by quicker the older I get, yet it also seems to slow and pool at other times. I have time to think and ponder more as I age, and with each passing season I have more to think about. Every now and then, I pull out one of my hunting journals and page through it, recounting past days, departed dogs, and hunts long past. One of the reasons old people tell stories is that they have lived long lives and have much to talk about. I could spend the next twenty-five years recounting my first twenty-five years of grouse and woodcock hunting. As I look back at these journals, at grouse fans propped up on bookshelves or at grouse tail feathers stuffed in old shell casings next to them, I see I have a lifetime of stories, a treasure of memories.

The older I grow the more I realize I'm hunting these stories and memories more than birds. With good health, I hope to hunt for another twenty-five years or longer, as long as I can plod along in the woods and point a shotgun. I have more stories to find and make.

Redemption Covert

As a kid growing up in a Baptist church, we often sang the old Frances Crosby hymn that began, "Redeemed, how I love to proclaim it! / Redeemed by the blood of the lamb." I had difficulty imagining a bloody lamb, but that's beside the point. It's a Baptist standard of sorts, and many congregants requested it during our frequent Sunday evening singalongs, shouting out its hymn number from the pews as if they were at an auction. *"Number 173!"* From the pulpit, we heard a lot about redemption, as various pastors and lay preachers pounded away at us sinners sitting in the pews with verses about redemption, grace, and mercy, so as a young boy I heard much about these abstract concepts. In Baptist theology, redemption always comes from God. There was nothing we could do to redeem our woe-begotten selves—that much I could understand. Then again, I was never much good at theology.

So, after not thinking about theology for years, it surprised me when I whispered "redemption" after tumbling a grouse on a gray November day in a Lincoln County covert. *Who said that?* I looked around, lifted my eyes up to the sky, and saw that I was alone. This hit came after a string of irritating misses—I've forgotten how many, but some fairly easy shots I usually make. Missing these gimmees really drove me nuts as a younger man. Years later, I have become more philosophical about my misses. Seeing a bird fly off to live another day isn't such a bad thing. But still . . .

Today, however, was different, with several misses piling up, misses at what should have been easy shots: hard points and birds coming up in range and in the spots where I expected them to be. The dog was doing his job—I wasn't. Finally, with that hit, with the bird in hand, I had redeemed myself and, I hoped, was back on track to shooting well. Hiking out of the woods, it struck me that redemption was something I had accomplished. An act of my will. I had redeemed myself, a concept foreign, as well as anathema, to my Baptist upbringing. Clearly, God was not a grouse or woodcock hunter who had experienced the sting of a long string of misses. Wandering around the woods these days, I think more and more about such things.

You unredeemed bastard," I yelled at Fergus after he bumped the fifth woodcock. It twittered away up and over the tops of the aspens. Five in a row—I was starting to lose my cool. These were woodcock, not a bird known for its cunning and trickery. *Five woodcock. Hell, even a puppy could point woodcock.* The birds Fergus had just bumped were sitting tightly as most woodcock do, not running as they will do on occasion. Fergus had walked right over the top of them as if either he couldn't smell them or he didn't care if he flushed them. I was beginning to think it was the latter. *Was he doing this to spite me?* Perhaps he didn't like the blankets in his kennel or he no longer liked the dog food he had been eating for seven years. Maybe he wanted to ride up in the cab instead of back in the box. Who knows? *A head cold? Did dogs get those?*

After the fifth bump, I picked up Fergus by the collar and hind end, set him back, and whoa-ed him. I kicked around the ground in front of the dog where the bird had been skulking, daring Fergus to flinch, then I picked up a stick and thrashed the brush with it in front of him just so he would know I was good and pissed. He stood his ground and looked at me, a defiant gleam in his eyes. Not only was he an unredeemed bastard, he was an unrepentant one as well.

"Did you take your cholesterol medicine today, honey?" Susan asked. "Maybe we should just go home. He's not going to get any

Fergus banished to the back of the truck. (Susan Parman)

better. We have all of those leaves to rake." She was tired of both of us—of Fergus's antics and my reaction to his behavior, which consisted mostly of me yelling at Fergus so he and anyone within a half mile could hear me.

It took two more spots and eight more bumped woodcock, for a total of thirteen, for me to finally call it a day. By then, I was hoarse and spent. I had no idea what had gotten into Fergus. He had never worked woodcock so poorly, even as a puppy. It was pathetic. *Maybe he really did have a head cold*, I thought as I slammed the tailgate and the topper door shut on him. No cab ride home for him today. His ears were flattened against his head and he pressed his nose up against the front topper window, pleading to ride up front with us. "A little too late, Buddy," I said as we backed up to turn around and head home.

Just before we reached the railroad tracks and the main highway home, we passed an aspen patch maybe one hundred yards square, bordered on three sides by what I call SPF, spruce pine fir. The trees looked about ten years old, the perfect age for holding woodcock. I slammed on the brakes and skidded to a halt, our dust overtaking the cab and billowing past. I stabbed the truck in reverse and ground backward. "Oh, no," was all Susan said. "Just one more try," I said. "I've always wanted to check this place out. It'll only take a few minutes."

I got out, while Susan said, "You go on. I'll make coffee for us." (We keep a camp stove and coffeepot in the back of the truck.) I jumped out, dropped the tailgate for Fergus, and set off into the popple.

We weren't halfway down the logging road through this cozy little covert when Fergus slammed into point. It was a thing of beauty and went a long way toward alleviating the agony of the rest of the morning. His head was lower than his outstretched tail, his sides heaving and nostrils flaring. He looked like a magazine cover, and I couldn't help but stand there and admire it for a moment.

As I inched by him, I searched the ground ahead for the wood-cock. Ten yards past the dog, white knuckles on my shotgun, I turned and circled back to the dog. He hadn't relaxed out of his magazine pose, and he didn't look up at me nor did he drop his tail, a sure sign the bird had flown. I did a 180 and worked away from Fergus, and fifteen or so yards out from him, a bird squirted between us.

If you have ever walked in on what you thought was a woodcock and a grouse thunders up, you can well imagine my surprise and understand how unnerving this is. It really does feel like holding onto an e-collar when your hunting buddy or significant other hits the juice, or like sticking a bobby pin in an electric outlet, which I once did as a kid on a dare from my brother. I had a scar on my thumb from this brilliant move for years. Still, I can't use that as an excuse for missing with both barrels on what was a relatively easy shot as far as grouse go. I blamed the miss on the red-hot adrenaline coursing through my bloodstream and my heart somewhere up in my throat. The bird banged up through the popple and cleared the trees, and the blue October sky backlit its gray form. It was a layup, a slam dunk, and I had missed. Twice.

When I slid into the driver's seat, Susan said, "Well?" I told her I had missed and turned the key in the ignition. "At least he finally pointed a woodcock." It was a grouse, I told her. "A grouse? And you missed?" Her smile almost cracked her face. And Fergus got to ride home up in the cab—on her lap, no less.

A month or so later, after the close of woodcock season, I turned off the highway and bumped over the tracks and passed the little aspen patch where I missed that easy shot. I thought briefly about pulling in and hunting it once again, figuring I might get another chance at that grouse, if Fergus could point and hold it as he did that day. But I wanted bigger and greener pastures, so I drove on down the road to another covert I had in mind.

We hunted a place I call Nose Lake a mile or so away. This place is mostly up and down, short, steep hills of aspen mixed with balsam fir. The balsams make for very effective screens, and it seems as if the grouse know precisely how to position themselves between the evergreens and the gun. They probably don't, but when they flush in a clatter of sound and fury, it seems they do.

According to my notes, we put up four birds, and I fired at two, missing them both. Fergus bumped one I would have had a good shot at. We arrived back at our parking spot with an empty game bag.

When we came back past the little aspen covert just before the highway, I pulled in and shut off the engine. *Why not?* I thought. *We're here.* The engine ticked as it cooled, and several moments passed until Fergus, eager to be off hunting, whined from the box. We got out and worked that little churchyard of a cover and passed what I thought was the spot where Fergus had redeemed himself and I had so ingloriously missed. We zigzagged to the east, then turned and worked the south edge along the SPF. Almost back to the road, twenty yards or so from the gravel, Fergus dropped into a point. Without hesitation, I ploughed straight ahead and past the dog and the bird came up. It flushed, quartering away from us right-to-left, not an especially difficult shot.

I tell myself it was the same bird—impossible to know for sure, but I like to think it was. Anyway, I never pulled the trigger and watched the bird fly up out of the popple and across the road and into the cover on the west side of the road. Often I will hold up on woodcock, but rarely do I do so with grouse. This one, however, I let go. I don't know why I didn't shoot at it. Regardless, it had been redeemed, as had we in our own way. I suppose the story would be better if I had centered it in a puff of feathers, but maybe not.

The final verse of Crosby's hymn goes like this: "I know there's a crown that is waiting / In yonder bright mansion for me, / And soon, with the spirits made perfect, / At home with the Lord I shall be." Baptist redemption never really appealed to me as a kid, in part because I wasn't into things like perfection, crowns of gold, and sparkling mansions. I still feel this way. We all have our versions of heaven, our own private theologies of what redemption looks and feels like. Mine features a cabin in the woods, a couple of setters, and a logging road leading through yellowing aspen, like the little church-yard of a covert we had just worked.

One would think this would also be a place where I never missed, where every shot produced a bird. But if that were the case, there would eventually be no grouse or woodcock left. Even a kid who daydreamed through most of his hours in church could understand this theology.

Serendipity

This doesn't happen often, I want to make that clear from the start. In fact, I can remember it happening only two or three times in all my years of grouse hunting. I get out of the truck, take a few steps, shoving shells in my shotgun and wondering what kind of day lies ahead, and before I get my head up, the air is full of birds. It's the stuff of dreams. A more likely scenario is hunting an hour or more before putting up the first bird.

But this was one of those days. Jenkins went on point while I was still shrugging into my vest. I grabbed my shotgun and hustled up to him. He was pointing along the ditch of the logging road we had driven in on, his head just in the edge of the cover. *No, this couldn't be. This never happens*, I thought. They could have been pecking gravel as we drove in past them. If so, how did I miss them?

Before I could get up to Jenkins, five or six birds burst into the air, an explosion of grouse. The rational side of my brain told my emotional body to keep calm: *Pick one out, don't shoot in the middle. Pick one out, don't shoot in the middle.* And for once, I listened to my rational mind and shot a bird peeling up and to the left and swung back and dropped one peeling off to the right and out over the road. Less than a minute into the hunt, and we had two birds down, their feathers floating silently, twirling back to earth. I stood there in that ancient stillness, not really believing what had just happened. But I quickly snapped out of my reverie and followed Jenkins after the first

Jenkins gets a whiff of an early season immature ruffed grouse. (Susan Parman)

bird, which had dropped down into some tag alders below us and the roadside. We found it shortly. The other bird had dropped in the road and fluttered the last of its life in the gravel and dust.

After collecting the second bird from the road, I took them back to the truck since it was only about twenty yards away. No need to carry them around all day, except as a warm reminder of what had just happened. I noted both were young gray birds, still coveyed up in the early season. What had I done? Shot two siblings, most likely, but I didn't let this thought dampen the third double of my grouse-hunting career. My Nutty Double, I dubbed it as I sat on the tailgate. Nutty was one of our nicknames for Jenkins, short for Nutter—he was a bit crazy as a pup. (He liked to attack furniture, a habit he has since outgrown.) Nutty Double sounded good, like the name of a candy bar, which held some truth since I had just been handed one big treat.

Serendipity has always played a major role in my hunting. Fifteen minutes before we showed up, this covey of birds could have been skulking deep in the tag alders or loafing across the road on private land where we don't have permission to hunt, but they just happened to be bunched up on the shoulder of the road as we passed by. We were in the right place at the right time, coincidental if you view the world as a cold, impersonal place, where events have no relationship to each other.

To me, however, those birds were a gift—they were serendipitous. I had done nothing to deserve them, other than pay attention to the dog and point my shotgun in the right direction. The still-warm bodies lying on my tailgate were not possessions I could earn or buy, like shrink-wrapped pork chops from Walmart. In the checkout line, we swipe a plastic card or insert it in the chip reader, and the clerk hands us the pork in a plastic bag. "Have a nice day," he says, holding out the receipt. Where had the pig lived and died? What had it eaten? Who had taken care of it?

I could understand the cost of the ruffed grouse just taken but not the price of factory-raised chickens. I had just subtracted two grouse from this corner of woods, changing it forever. So even though part of me wanted to dance a jig because of my double, another part of me understood the gravity of taking those two young birds, subtracting them from the woods forever. How do we understand the contradiction of this moment of intense primitive joy and awful regret? This is the paradox, some people say, the problem of hunting, this bloody taking of life.

After clicking shut the tailgate, I grabbed my shotgun and we worked down the creek past the tag alders, following up the birds from the Serendipity Flush. A hundred or so yards down the creek, up on the shallow ridge of its southern bank, a bird flushed wild and planed across the creek, safe for another day. I stopped in my tracks, as did Jenkins to my right. He hadn't run into the scent cone of the bird, but he stopped when he heard the flush. Just as I was about to take a step and move on, I noticed a grouse perching in the lowest branch of a hemlock about head high, eye level. It cocked its head around nervously and lengthened its body into a skinny pole. The tufts of feathers on the crest of its head looked like a Mohawk haircut. By now, Jenkins had spied it and emitted a low growl.

"*Shoo!*" I yelled, but the bird just perched there like a ticking time bomb about to go off. "*Shoo!*" I yelled and stepped toward the bird. It launched up into the green of the next lowest branch and scrambled to make speed as I brought my gun up. It launched itself into the clear-cut running up the hill. When the barrels caught up to the bird, I passed them through its body without pulling the trigger and watched it fly away. It seemed hoggish and not all that sporting to shoot a bird right after a double.

I don't know why I followed the bird up the hill to an old barbwire fence that marked where the public land ended. I didn't intend to shoot it, but I followed anyway. I couldn't continue to chase it across the fence line onto private land. Mostly I seemed to be trailing along after the dog, who couldn't read the No Trespassing signs. He didn't intend for it to get away.

An old pasture lay on the far side of the fence, and crabapple trees grew all up and down the rusty barbwire. A few crabapples had also moved into and colonized the old pasture. Grouse love to eat the gnarly apples as well as dine on the buds in winter.

Years ago when I walked down the fence line on the public side, at least a dozen birds loaded down with crabapples busted out from underneath these trees. I shot one as it flushed my way, its crop crammed full of windfall apples. Whenever I hunt here, I make a pass down the fence line and hope to see that glorious sight once again, but it happened only that one time. The trees usually hold a bird or two, sometimes none, but never that grand flush. These days the few that flush usually veer south away from the fence line and the public land and beat it across the small pasture to the tree line on the far side. Rarely do they flush back onto the public side, where I can get a shot at them. They seem to know where their safety lies.

This one didn't. It burst out of the crabapples behind me and churned down the fence line back toward the logging road where all of my luck had started. We continued to follow it. I didn't need to coax Jenkins into doing so. When we pushed out of the woods to the road, I figured the bird had probably turned back over the fence onto the private land, which was old mature woods and no longer pasture out by the road.

We worked around the cover adjacent to the road, but it seemed the bird had escaped, so we turned right and headed back toward our parking spot. I wouldn't have to make a decision about taking another bird.

Halfway back, Jenkins started to make game and quickly locked down into a point. He was in the ditch again, just off the road, not unlike the point with which we began our hunt. I came up past him into the brushy clear-cut and made a big circle out in front of him, then worked back to the dog. His tail had dropped by the time I got back to him, and he looked at me with a question in his eyes. "Where's the bird?" I tapped him on the head and he dove into the woods. I walked out onto the road, from where I watched him work, and when he had been through the area thoroughly, I called him back to me.

Jenkins wanted to jump back into the woods and hunt some more, but I heeled him down the road. We had had a good day. It was time to go home. He protested and looked longingly at the cover on our right, but I kept him at my side. When we passed a scrubby bush on our left, I noticed the form out the corner of my eye just before it lifted off. The sound of a grouse flush is unmistakable. Whirling toward the noise, I watched the bird bore across another pasture, this one a good half mile across. It's an unusually large pasture for the Northwoods, and several dozen Herefords, an uncommon cow for here as well, grazed placidly in the lush green grass.

It bored across the pasture until I lost it in the grays and browns of the far tree line. It vanished into the woods, into some other country. It, too, had a lucky day.

The Singing Fields

The Singing Fields, each meadow about three or four acres, are cut into and surrounded by acres of aspen. These aspen trees, as I write, are of the particular age woodcock love, eight to ten years old, whippy trees about the diameter of the fat end of a pool cue. Balsam fir mix in here and there, and an occasional mature white pine stands a lonely sentinel on the highest ground. Ever since I came across these two clear-cuts, I have been waiting patiently for the cover to age to perfection like a good wine or cheese. Soon enough, the trees will mature beyond prime cover, thinning out and those left growing stouter and taller, and the woodcock will move on to better cover. But in the meantime, savor the moment.

Moist lowlands border the popple surrounding the Singing Fields, and most of the woodcock like to loaf down in the wetter places of the edge cover. Both fields sit high and dry on the upland, sloping down through the popples to the seeps of water and tag alders there. In wet conditions, I wear rubber boots, such boots often a compromise when grouse and woodcock hunting since they don't walk well the miles necessary to hunt these birds. On the other hand, I do like dry feet and loathe water squishing between my toes.

We found the Singing Fields haphazardly, like most of our coverts. One hunt we simply followed a faint logging road never taken just to see where it led—and it took us over a shallow hill and dropped down into the first of the fields, surrounded at that time by bald

Susan and Jenkins at the Woodcock Rock with three woodcock. (Mark Parman)

clear-cut. Through the clear-cut to the south, we could see the second field.

Some years later, after the popple had matured, we came back for our first hunt, and by the time we had worked the edge around the perimeter of the first field, we each had a limit of woodcock. The next hunt here, we hunted the second field, also filled with woodcock—and one grouse, which I missed. We were down in the tag alders, the dog on point, and the grouse came up. We were thinking woodcock, and we got an unexpected grouse, which always compounds the difficult shooting of these birds. Expecting a curveball, the fastball blew right by us. Still, that fleeing grouse was a good sign. Maybe we would be ready next time, too.

These fields are intentional openings, kept open by the county's frequent mowing. Without that, the aspen would colonize the openings and take over, and the fields would disappear, resulting in a massive monoculture, and most likely fewer woodcock. If I owned a large aspen stand, I would create openings just like this. In fall, I would have birds to hunt; in spring, we could watch and listen to the woodcock's sky dance—their twirling acrobatics in the April chill and their fluty, liquid notes. Their dance alone would be worth keeping the fields open. We dream of someday owning a Singing Field.

But this isn't merely a story about shooting woodcock, since much of it happened after the woodcock season had closed and just before Wisconsin's nine-day gun deer season. It was unseasonably warm weather for mid-November with highs approaching fifty. With the warm temps, I was curious if a few woodcock would still be hanging around, and if so, maybe get some pictures of the dog on point. But more so, I wanted to explore the popple on the north side of the seep bordering the Singing Fields—and maybe shoot a grouse or two if any were lurking around.

This story really starts with a race I ran the morning of this narrative, a 2.5-mile run up Rib Mountain in Wausau, but Susan says I'm just forgetful—all the time and not just after running and I'm oxygen deprived. We got out of the truck and were gearing up when I realized I had forgotten my shotgun back home. I had grabbed Susan's gun case, which looks just like mine, and she figured I was being a gentleman and carrying her gun to the truck when we loaded up and never said anything. As we were forty or so miles from home when we discovered my mistake, turning around and going back for my gun wasn't realistic. The November sun was already low on the horizon.

I said I would carry the camera and get some pictures, but Susan said we could take turns using her Benelli. This might not have been such a discouraging event—and a humorous one now looking back— if we were both right-handed. But we're not. As I said earlier, I have the unfortunate handicap of being left-handed. As we started out, Susan graciously suggested I take the first turn and handed me her shotgun.

We worked into the new cover, and shortly Fergus was on point on a low ridge topped by several mature aspen trees. As I walked in on the point under these trees where it was fairly clear, I reminded myself that the safety slid in the opposite direction of my left-handed Benelli. I wanted to flick it off while moving in on the bird, but decided safety first. I could trip and shoot my foot, the dog, who knows, maybe even Susan behind me. Stranger accidents have occurred.

At any rate, I worked a circle out in front of Fergus and then back to his side as he continued to hold point, the feathering on his legs and tail flagging in the breeze. His nostrils quivered with the scent. I was just about to say something to Susan, like *I think the bird flushed before we got here*, when a ruffed grouse bolted out of one of the mature aspens overhead. It was a good twenty feet up in that tree when it flushed. I fumbled with the safety, threw the gun in the general direction of the bird, and wasted two shells.

"My turn," Susan said as the shots echoed around the hills, and reached out for her gun.

"No fair. That shot was impossible."

"It's my turn. I let you go first and you missed. Big time. It's my turn." So I manned up and handed *her* gun over.

We debated following up my missed bird, but it was up high and flying hard when it disappeared, so instead we worked in the opposite direction and down off the low ridge through young and nearly impenetrable aspen toward another seep of clotted tag alders. Fergus starting making game as he moved toward the tags and then eased into a point. Susan, gun at the ready, worked toward the dog on his left side, and I approached on the right with the camera.

When Susan was nearly even with the dog, a grouse burst out on her left, and as the bird cleared the trees and banked back to the right showing its mottled breast feathers, she tumbled it. The bird cartwheeled several times and caromed off the trees. As it hit the ground, a second bird came up in front of me, and Susan pivoted right and shot once and missed.

I couldn't remember the last time I had stood back and witnessed a grouse hunt *gunless*. I often watch others shoot woodcock but never sit back when grouse are the game. There was the bird hanging like a zeppelin ten yards in front of me, and all I had to point in its direction was a camera. Despite all the action, I hadn't taken a single shot with the camera. I couldn't work a right-handed safety and was even more awkward at crunch time with the camera.

We worked through the rest of the cover and then cut the main logging road without another point. As we moved through the tags, we bantered about whether Susan would have had a true double and whether I would get to shoot at the next two birds since she had taken two shots. As we walked down the logging road east toward another cover, I maintained that it wasn't a true double since both birds were not in the air at the same time, and that two shots were two shots. Fair's fair. Susan felt otherwise. I did have the shotgun in my hands.

At the entrance to the next cover, we were slipping through the boulders blocking the logging road from vehicle access off a gravel road when a bird burst up between my feet. Fergus was downwind working over the popples on our right and had completely missed the grouse hunkering in the middle of the trail. I'm always shocked that we can't see birds that close to us, but you can't see what you're not looking for.

I swung on the rising bird and pulled—once, twice, three times—and yet the trigger refused to budge. I'm surprised I didn't bend it I pulled so hard. I had pushed the safety to the right (reflex for a lefty), which was the On position. As the bird flew up the hill and out of sight, Susan was laughing so hard she couldn't speak for a few moments. Fergus loped over to see what was going on and got a nose full of grouse and flashed a point. I swatted him in the ass and said, "Nice going. Now you smell it. It's gone, you idiot." "Don't blame him," said Susan, still laughing.

I sweet-talked Susan into another turn, arguing that technically I hadn't fired, and she acquiesced, feeling sorry for me, no doubt. We continued on the logging road up the hill and down the other side while Fergus worked the cover, this time on both sides of the trail. At the lowest point on the other side of the hill, Fergus locked down in a point a couple of dog lengths into the aspen. I hustled up to him, and as I did searched the bare woods floor for birds. *Fool me once.* Remarkably, I spotted the forms of two grouse just as they lifted off the ground in the thunder of their wings. I focused on the one closest, swung on it, and this time managed to flick the safety off before I pulled the trigger. Feathers puffed on my first shot as it cleared the treetops, but the bird kept on flying so I fired again. I expected it to drop, but it kept on flying.

If that Benelli had been mine, I might have swung it at the nearest big tree. It had been an easy shot, one that I typically make, and *that gun* missed. *What kind of shells were we using? Cheap Walmart ones?* I looked over at Susan, who was trying not to laugh. "It's not funny," I said.

I handed the shotgun to Susan, and we followed after the hit bird. Clearly it was wounded. After my shots, I had caught a breast feather as it floated twirling down out of the sky like a fat snowflake. I like to follow all birds I shoot at, since I have recovered numerous dead birds over the years, even ones looking like clean misses. This was not a clean miss, however, but it obviously wasn't a clean hit either. I didn't want to think about a wounded bird, the blood on my hands, but there it was.

A hundred or so yards past where I had taken my shots, Fergus started to make game and shortly went on point. We circled around the dog, Susan ready to shoot and me with my eyes scanning the ground for the dead or injured bird. The camera was now an after-thought. I was just about to declare it a false point when I noticed a single gray-phased tail feather a few yards in front of Fergus's nose. After I picked it up, I tapped him on the head and told him to move on. We worked the immediate area around the point, covering all the high ground that eventually dead-ended at a low marsh. I was fairly confident the bird had reflushed across this marsh and perhaps had a chance to survive. Even so, I wished I had either hit or missed it cleanly, but that is not how hunting works.

We worked out of the cover and back to the trail, only to discover yet another intersection and another trail leading to another aspen cutting that looked worth hunting someday. But as it was getting toward sunset, we turned around and headed back toward our truck, vowing to return and check out this new territory.

Returning two days before gun deer season, I explored the new cover, discovering yet two more huge cuttings. I shot two grouse, hoping one was the injured bird, but I'll never know. I also found a third field. We would return here the following autumn—this time with *two* shotguns.

Storybook Covert

We had let the dog out of the truck before we were ready to hunt—a cardinal sin of sorts, I suppose—and were getting rid of the coffee we had drunk on the forty-five-minute drive up to one of our favorite covers. I thought the dog was doing the same, lifting his leg high on some weeds, emptying himself before the hunt, but when I caught him out of the corner of my eye, I suddenly realized he was on point. It was a jolt more potent than all the caffeine we had swigged that morning. I zipped up, grabbed my case, fumbled with that zipper, frantically sliding in two shells, making sure they were brass side up, and half ran over to Fergus, our older English setter.

As I came up, he relocated a step to his right, then repointed, and I walked around him on his left. His sides and flews were heaving. This was serious. When I got a few steps past his outstretched body, a grouse exploded out of the head-high brush and bolted for the trees bordering the fence line of the gravel road twenty yards to our right. A left-to-right crosser in the clear, about as easy as shots come in the grouse woods. I was so close to the bird, I could see it was a brown-phased grouse. I made sure to swing well ahead of the charging bird and pulled the trigger. Fully expecting it to tumble, I was stunned when the bird kept flying through the popple trees along the road and into the cover on the north side of road. Maybe that bird was wearing a flak jacket.

I stood there staring at the tree line until Susan came up and asked, "How did you miss that one?" I didn't know if she was mocking me or asking a legitimate question, but I thought, *High? Low? Behind it? Surely I was not in front of it?* Such a gift—and I let it get away. I was so surprised at missing, I never even fired the second barrel. I wanted to pack the dog and ourselves back into the truck and drive home to spend the rest of the day on the couch staring at college football on TV, and perhaps I would have if it weren't for Susan and Fergus. Instead I shrugged into my vest and we slipped into the woods, trailing after the tinkle of Fergus's bell.

In the next hour, Fergus pointed three more grouse, but we didn't get any clear shots. The grouse were holed up in the thickest of the cover—tag alders mixed with dense popple, the age of cutting you have to turn sideways to force your way through. The fleeting glimpse of these three birds through the green curtain only increased my regret at missing the first in the clear blue of the Wisconsin sky. *How could I have missed that bird?* It was gnawing away at me.

"That bird has to be in there somewhere," I said, pointing to the cover on the north side of the road, when we returned to the truck. That first bird had flushed over there somewhere. "You don't mind if we hunt that a bit, do you?" I asked.

Susan said something like, "As in you two"—pointing at Fergus—"or the three of us?"

"You can come if you like." She shot me a look that didn't inspire confidence but picked up her shotgun and crossed the road with me. It didn't take Fergus long to go on point, and when the bird flushed I threw a shot after it, but it too was fleeing through heavy cover. I couldn't be sure, but it looked like a gray-phased bird, not the first one I had so ingloriously missed. After this last miss, I was thoroughly dejected, and so we swung around toward the truck. It was time to call it a day.

Just a few moments later, Fergus flashed a point, took a few steps, and flashed another. Then he nosed around on the ground. "Look," Susan yelled, pointing to a dead bird lying neatly in the leaves. A dead brown bird. No, it couldn't be. I picked it up as Fergus moved on to find more live game. It was still somewhat warm. It had been dead only a short while. *Could it be?* I wondered. Examining the body, I couldn't find marks from a predator or any signs of harm for that matter, but I still didn't believe this was the bird I had shot at right out of the truck.

"Its head was pointing in the direction of the road," Susan noted. It had been flying in the opposite direction, dead north. How did it come to rest that way, pointing south? I figured if it had died in the air, it could have bounced and ended up facing south. Who knows, I thought, and slipped the dead bird into my game vest, figuring this grouse would taste wonderful no matter how it had died.

When we got home later that day and I had cleaned the bird, the mystery was solved. It had taken two pellets to the head and at least one to the neck. That grouse had taken those hits and probably died in the air somewhere beyond the tree line, out of sight and out of mind. I hadn't missed it after all, and what I had thought was a spectacular miss had been only the beginning of a story.

I call this covert Storybook, not because it is some kind of fantasyland of endless birds, a place where the dogs always point and the hunters never miss. The place gets its name from the stories it seems to generate. Like the flak-jacket grouse, or the following one, for instance.

We were hunting up a hollow, struggling up the hill through a stand of young aspen. When we broke through that into what I had hoped would be a clearing at the top of a small rise, we found ourselves tangled in what around here reminds me of the Briar Patch. It's exactly the place where the grouse wants to get thrown—"Oh please don't throw me into that blackberry patch." The canes were about the same diameter as nickels, and the thorns as sharp as the teeth of a young puppy or a northern pike.

Of course, Fergus goes on point in the middle of this berry patch. When I squatted down and got beneath most of the leaves, I could see him ahead locked on scent. I looked at Susan and she looked at me, and I said, "OK, I'm going in." You pretty much abandon all hope when you go into a patch like this. I put my head down and bulled my way toward the dog, the briars grabbing and ripping my shirt, my vest, my pants, my hands, my face. Halfway to the dog, my hat got ripped off. (Someday, I'm going to invent one with a chinstrap.) I kept on, bareheaded.

Before I got up to Fergus, birds started to flush out of the berries, maybe three or four; I couldn't tell in the midst of all that tangle. Susan shot on my left. As I ripped my shotgun free of the berry brambles, the final bird flushed and headed straightaway into the sun. It was sort of like trying to shoot when someone was trying to lasso you and while you were staring into the high beams of an oncoming car. Nevertheless, I got off both barrels. I was sure I hadn't even nicked a feather of this last grouse, pretty clear from the way it bored straight east, destination Tomahawk, five or so miles away as the crow—or in this case the grouse—flies. It was at least a hundred yards out, not much more than a speck on the horizon, when it suddenly turned and soared up into the clear October sky like it wanted to join the contrails overhead. I had never seen a bird fly straight up like that and haven't since. It went about as high as male woodcocks ascend during the sky dance, but they spiral up into the sky. Vultures and raptors wheeled around, riding the thermals to gain altitude. This grouse climbed like it was a fighter jet.

I thought the bird had lost its mind—or had it shot out—but then I recalled a Burton Spiller story about a towering bird. According to Spiller, a bird towers when it gets shot in the eye, and since it cannot see, it flies directly up to avoid earthbound obstacles. When I read the story at the time, I thought it was just that—a good story. In all my years of grouse hunting, I had never seen a bird "tower." Besides, those old writers at times liked to exaggerate.

At any rate, that grouse kept climbing and climbing into the heavens, and we stood there on that hill watching. It climbed a bit more, then hesitated and folded its wings, dropping head first like a stone. It crash-landed not far from where we had parked. I looked at Susan to see if she was seeing what I had just seen. She had.

I'm usually poor at marking where birds fall. When I knock down a grouse, I often say to myself, *Wow, did I just hit that bird?* or I might watch the way the feathers twirl down to earth like the falling leaves of aspen or maple. Instead, I should be marking them, but luckily, shot grouse are not hard to find. They don't run when wounded like pheasants or slip down a hole like quail. Marking this grouse, however, was impossible since the bird had dropped so far from us. I tried to get a fix on a nearby tree, but it had dropped into yet another aspen cutting, where one tree looks exactly like the thousands of others around it.

Knowing the bird was dead (it couldn't have survived its freefall), we searched for it on both sides of the road where it looked to have fallen. When we had thoroughly combed over both sides of the road, we started all over and did it again. Susan gave up first and lit the camp stove for coffee while I searched a third and final time. Finally, I gave up and returned to the truck, emptyhanded.

While sipping coffee on the tailgate, we didn't realize Fergus had slipped away. I walked around to the front of the truck, wondering where he could have gone to, and there he stood—on point maybe ten yards into popple. I ran back, got my shotgun, and made my way back to the dog, praying the bird would hold.

I got up to him and there lay a dead grouse a few feet in front of him, wings outstretched, looking like a glider that had softly crash-landed, not one that had nose-dived. It looked peaceful, as if it were sleeping. I picked it up and let Fergus sniff it awhile before I handed it to Susan, who had followed me around the truck. "The towering bird," I said. "Maybe those old guys knew what they were talking about."

When we got home, I autopsied this bird as well. I hadn't hit either of its eyes, nor could I find any shot in the head or the body. It would be a good eater, the breast unharmed. We decided it died of either cardiac arrest or possibly old age.

The third story: We had both dogs on the ground, which is some-times not a good idea, such as this day. Both were working too far out, competing with each other, making it difficult to hear their bells and track their whereabouts. That far away, it was also impossible to see them work. They were not the perfectly matched brace of setters one would expect to find in a place called Storybook.

Just as I called them in, blowing so hard on the whistle my face turned purple, Susan yelled something indistinct on my left and fired twice. The shots brought the dogs running. I made my way over to Susan through the young aspen, and she asked me if I saw the bird go down. "Go down?" I asked. "I never saw it get up." She said it had burst up right between her legs, and she was mad at the dogs for being so far off and self-hunting.

She insisted she had knocked the grouse down, and I believed her. So I brought the dogs over and commanded them to hunt dead. They searched for several minutes before Jenkins flashed a point, and I kicked around the withered grass and sticks and slash until he even-tually gave up and moved on. The dogs started to work away from us, as they clearly wanted to keep moving, but I called them back and told them to look some more. "Are you sure you hit it?" I asked. Susan was positive she saw it tumble, but she must have seen doubt creeping over my face. "You don't believe me, do you?"

Jenkins flashed another point where he had a few moments earlier, so we went back to that spot. Standing there, the brown bar of a grouse feather materialized like a Rorschach pattern out of the background of forest duff. Just one feather lying there. She did hit it after all. I bent down to pick it up, but when I tried, it was attached to a fan full of feathers, which, in turn, was attached to a bird. One feather was sticking out over a branch the bird had crawled under before it died. I pulled it out and let Jenkins stick his muzzle in the still warm breast feathers before handing it to Susan. Stroking the blood-stained breast feathers she said, "See, I told you I hit it." I told her I had never doubted her for a single moment. It was a good thing I saw that one tail feather lying there.

Jenkins crowds Fergus, as Mark fans out a grouse tail. (Susan Parman)

At Storybook, we make sure to follow up every bird we fire at, even if it looks like it flew into the next county. Regardless of place, it's good practice to go after each and every bird we shoot at. Here we never know what we'll find, but for sure, a good story.

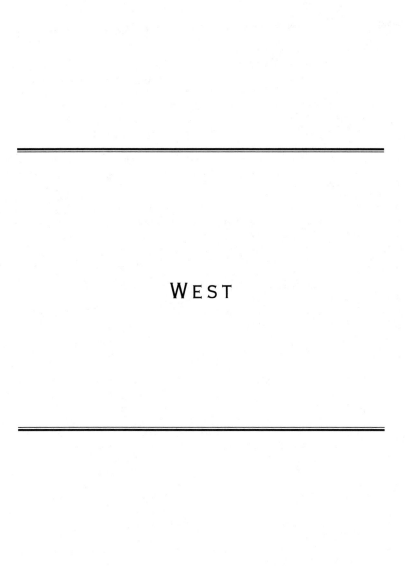

WEST

The Bermuda Triangle

I couldn't quite put my finger on why I didn't like the place we had just hunted, but something there made me uneasy. Several years earlier, I had noticed this covert while driving by on my way to a somewhere-else covert. I made a mental note to mark it on my map as a potential covert. Today, I had finally returned to check it out.

A few minutes of walking into this new spot, the ground spongy beneath my feet, I had a bad feeling someone or something was watching me. I kept looking back over my shoulder, my head on a swivel. The dog, up ahead working the cover, didn't seem spooked— this was just another fine place to hunt for him. I had to resist turning around and returning to my truck, the coffee still warm in my travel mug, but I pressed on, hoping my anxiety would lift. It never did.

I tried to understand the cause of my anxiety. Was it the improbable symmetry of all the tree trunks with their perfect spacing, an odd, barely perceptible scent in the air, or the ancient claustrophobia of a primate who evolved on the savannah? I couldn't say. The place was just bad, and I knew I wouldn't return, but the nail in the coffin was a lone grouse flush in over two hours of trudging. Had we put up more birds maybe I would have felt differently about the place. Getting lots of birds changes things, and I would have worked it into my repertoire of coverts and ignored the bad feeling. Instead, when I got back to the truck, I crossed it out on my map.

In my searching for new coverts over the years, I have run across a half dozen of what I call "voodoo coverts." They look good on paper or on a USGS or Google map, but on the ground they quickly reveal themselves as something else. Most of them I avoid, never to return—going there once was enough to convince me to stay away forever—but I do return to a few of these voodoo coverts, against my better intuition, because they reliably hold birds.

Take the Bermuda Triangle. It's one of my best coverts, even though over the years the place has tried its best to maim and kill us. This place is hazardous to our health, exacting a price for entry. Nevertheless, we return, willing to accept whatever the place throws at us because we always see, and usually shoot, grouse here. The Bermuda Triangle demands a price, but it's one we're willing to pay.

When Susan picked herself up and looked at her finger, she nearly threw up, which is saying a lot since she is a surgical nurse. She has seen hearts beating in chests held open with retractors; she has heard the whine of saws cutting through bone; she has smelled the foulness of infection or cauterized flesh. Blood and gore are her typical and daily fare, but it is different when the bloody wound is attached to your own person, something you can hold up to your eyes, while feeling the throbbing agony. I can attest her face was as white as this paper, the blood perhaps running out her face and dripping out her finger.

She had stumbled on top of a ridge of mature maples (as open as it gets in the grouse woods) trying to scramble down to Fergus, who had struck a point below us along the edge of a young aspen cutting. It was the perfect place to catch a grouse napping, warm and sunny with a backdrop of cover. It's likely the longer grass underneath the maples camouflaged the slash or stone that tripped her, but why she fell isn't as important as how she fell—directly on top of an ottoman-sized chunk of granite. Her ring finger was underneath the trigger guard of her Ugartechea, and she landed with all her weight on the shotgun. It was like dropping an anvil on the tip of her finger.

Fergus on stylish point in the Bermuda Triangle. (Susan Parman)

The crushing impact blew off the fingernail, leaving the cuticle exposed and bloody. My brother was with us and hunting closest to her, and he yelled at me to come quick as I was down by Fergus, still holding his point, waiting for me to flush the bird. I quickly flushed the bird—a woodcock—and ran back up the hill. I could hear panic in his voice. Seeing my brother's face confirmed that something was wrong. I don't work in an operating room, so I have no problem admitting I almost lost my breakfast coffee and oatmeal when I saw her finger. Susan was in so much pain she was dancing in place, holding her hand above her head. I broke down her side-by-side and shoved the three pieces in my game bag, and we started the hour-long march out of the woods and back to the truck.

From the parking lot, it was another forty-five minutes to the ER, Susan keeping her hand elevated in the back seat to minimize the throbbing. According to Susan, the impact blew up her finger "like a ballpark frank." It split her finger and pulverized the bone into dozens of shards. In the ER, a digital nerve block eased the pain as the doctor picked out fragments of bone and sewed her up. She took a few weeks off after that and bought a new shotgun, for good measure.

Ten years earlier and maybe two hundred yards away from Susan's incident, I got my first taste of what the Bermuda Triangle could dish out. This spot became the second point of the triangle. I tripped and somersaulted down the same ridge a little farther north while trying to get to a pointed bird our now dead setter Ox was holding. I did a complete three-sixty through a blackberry patch and landed on my feet, gun still at port arms. The blackberry canes helped slow my fall and kept me from striking the ground. *Well, that was slick*, I said to myself. *Too bad nobody witnessed that because no one will believe me when I tell them.* Stunned that I was not dangling an arm or a leg or paralyzed from the neck down, I checked my shotgun, then headed toward the dog. I don't even remember if I shot the bird Ox was pointing. I should have realized this near catastrophe was a warning.

Falls are inevitable while grouse hunting. The woods floor is clotted with blowdown and logging slash, the surface uneven. Stones and roots grab your boots, while vines and brambles try to wrap up your feet. I often fall when approaching a grouse point, because I'm always hurrying up to the dog, heedless of the terrain. Grouse are typically jumpy and refuse to wait around for a hunter to get a good shot. They don't sit tightly like woodcock, and because I close in on a point with my head up, not looking down at where I'm planting my feet—well, that's a recipe for a fall. If I looked down at my boots, I wouldn't fall nearly as often, but I wouldn't get as many good looks at grouse. Holding on to a shotgun with both hands also affects our balance, increasing spills. If I were simply hiking through the woods with a walking stick, I would be much less apt to fall, much safer, but it wouldn't be nearly as exciting. The shotgun in my hands changes everything.

The third point of the triangle lies about a half mile to the south and earned this distinction after I received a black eye from a hostile popple whip. This happened just a few weeks after Susan's mishap, so I was hunting alone, her injury effectively ending her season. With her finger in a soft cast, there was no way for her to hold a shotgun or to pull its trigger. She did follow along a few times with a camera, but not this day. Once again, I was trying to hustle up to the dog on point. I heard a bird lift off as I made my way up to the dog, so instead of wisely going under a two-inch branch, I tried to push through it with my free right hand in case there was more than one bird. When it was under pressure, it snapped off and the part still connected to the tree whipped back and smacked me in the face and knocked me down. Adding insult to my injury, as I lay there, hand to my watering eye and groveling in the leaves, what sounded like a half-dozen birds flushed. It didn't matter. Had I been on my feet, I couldn't have seen to shoot anyway.

When I got home, it looked as if I had been in a bar fight. Susan was so impressed she took a picture of my shiner, perhaps in part because I had taken pictures of her finger. Touché.

From the air, the Bermuda Triangle would look more like a skinny piece of pie with two long sides and one short one than an isosceles triangle. Unlike the Bermuda Triangle or, say, Area 51, no planes have disappeared here, no UFOs have been sighted—at least none that I know of; it's simply a place where we've had an unusual number of accidents. I try to be careful here, and Susan once suggested I wear one of my motorcycle or bicycle helmets when hunting here. However, I don't own one in blaze orange, and I don't know how I would explain my looks if I ran into another hunter. We keep returning here, however, because we have good luck with the hunting. Here, the birds, both grouse and woodcock, consistently offer themselves up to us.

Hunting is often about luck, both bad and good luck. In Richard Nelson's book *The Island Within*, he wrote of the Koyukon view of how hunters' thoughts and actions shape and influence their luck. Grandpa William, an old Koyukon hunter, said to Nelson: "A good hunter . . . that's somebody the animals *come* to. But if you lose your luck with a certain kind of animal—maybe you talk wrong about it or don't treat it with respect—then for a while you won't get any, not matter how hard you try." This idea of treating prey with respect and how this affects our luck runs through most Native American hunting traditions, but not the mainstream American tradition, which focuses on technology and individual skill.

How do we explain the deep mysteries of luck, especially in a scientific and materialistic age such as ours? Despite the fact that hunters place an inordinate amount of faith in gadgets or in their own ability, hunting often comes down to a matter of luck, both good and bad. How else do I explain tripping on a smooth logging road as I pivot to face a grouse flying in the clear down the open corridor of the road? How do I explain a single erratically flying piece of #8 shot that just happened to penetrate the breast and lodge in the bird's heart? How do I explain a grouse flushing from the exact spot at the base of a massive white pine that a bird flushed from four hours earlier as I was setting out on my hunt? I was so astounded by this miraculous flush I surprised myself by actually dropping the bird. Who would believe this? Some days even I doubt what happens to me in the woods.

Over the years, I've carried several lucky charms in my vest pockets. Twenty years ago, I picked up a spent 16 gauge cartridge in the woods since it was the first one I had ever seen. I had a good day of hunting and shot a few birds, so I kept the shell in my vest pocket for good luck. It rattled around in this pocket for a couple of seasons until I lost it one day after pulling out my compass, some live shells, or a Jolly Rancher. Whatever the reason, my good-luck charm was gone.

After the 16 gauge shell, I carried around a walnut, heavily polished from handling it so often. It came from the only walnut tree I know that grows in my string of coverts, but I lost that nut after some time as well. Typically, I keep an array of grouse and woodcock tail feathers in my vest pockets, where they get frayed and battered and need refreshing from time to time, but this means I'm shooting birds and thus proves their worth as good-luck charms. Whatever it might be, I need something in my pocket for luck.

I know a hunter who wears a lucky hat and insists it was responsible for a double he shot. It looks like the double was back in 1985. I, too, have favorite hats but don't endow them with any special good fortune—yet. I'm sure other hunters wear lucky socks, lucky shirts, lucky pants; others might bring along a gun handed down to them from a father, an uncle, an old friend. "Uncle Jim was a crack shot. I hope some of his luck is still on this gun and rubs off on me." If Uncle Jim was five feet six inches and his nephew six feet two inches, good luck, because even good luck has difficulties compensating for poor gun fit.

More than amulets and talismans, I put stock in the respect I show to grouse and the hunting rituals I have unconsciously adopted over the years. This is why I don't shoot them out of trees or on the ground. Others may do so, but my taboos are for me and only affect my hunting. I don't like to call ruffed grouse "timber chickens" or "fool's hens" because this disrespects the bird. I don't like to go after drumming birds—which other hunters tell me is folly anyway—because it seems unfair to shoot a bird blinded by lust or simply protecting its territory. I don't like to take more than my fair share of birds from one covert, which probably makes no sense whatsoever because nearly all my coverts are on public land and others can and do hunt there, taking as many birds as they see fit. My numbers are arbitrary at best. I like to treat dead grouse with the reverence they're due, and I don't heave them in the back of my truck or clean one by stepping on the wings and wrenching the body apart by yanking on the legs. I have a hard time throwing away grouse fans and therefore have dozens stashed around the house, up at our cabin, in my office, and in my truck. I stick to my rituals, hoping and praying to keep on the good side of the ruffed grouse so a few may always lie well in front of the dog, flush at my step, and offer the chance of a shot.

When it comes to grouse hunting, like many of the good things in life, you can never have too much good luck.

Berry Covert

The scratched and bloody backs of my hands attest to the many berry patches I thrash through while grouse hunting. Some time ago, I was racing downhill to a point, tripped in a dense, nearly impenetrable patch of blackberries as I dropped down to the dog—the canes at their bases the diameter of a nickel—and cartwheeled head over heels. The canes, however, were so thick they cushioned my fall and held me above ground like a mattress, and there I was, lying on my thorny bed, still gripping my shotgun. Other than a few more scratches I was fine, so I extricated myself as quickly as possible in that tangle and found the dog still on point, an event I wrote about in the essay "The Bermuda Triangle."

This covert and this essay, however, are not about thorny berries, although there are plenty of pockets of nasty old canes here. Rather, they are named after an idea of Wendell Berry, a Kentucky farmer and author. Berry writes in his poem "Manifesto: The Mad Farmer Liberation Front": "So, friends, every day do something that won't compute." This poem belongs to a cycle attributed to Berry's Mad Farmer, a cranky contrarian, whose wisdom and wit go against the grain of our modern world. If the Mad Farmer lived in northern Wisconsin, he might on occasion follow a dog through the woods, his gnarly hands gripping an old battered Parker, doing something that would never compute in modern agribusiness economics.

Grouse and woodcock hunting rarely computes, not in dollars and cents, not in our mad rush to "get ahead" at all costs. If time is money, and money is all that matters, then it's best we stay out of the woods, out of the fields, and off the waters. Keep your nose to the grindstone, chasing money.

Even if it were possible, I really don't care to calculate what a pound of grouse or woodcock flesh costs because doing so would be beside the point. If I did, however, try to determine its true cost, I would need to add up all my equipment costs: shotguns, shells, brush pants, vests, blaze-orange hats, boots, and all the worn-out pairs of boots. (I threw a pair out just the other day.) Then there are the license fees, although the in-state Wisconsin small-game license at a mere eighteen dollars is one of the best values around. Dog food, dog treats, dog beds, dog toys, vet bills, kennels, and collars—those canines aren't cheap. And I can't forget to add in all the driving to my coverts scattered around three or four north-central Wisconsin counties. At fifty-five cents a mile, that adds up quickly. I'm sure I've forgotten numerous other expenses, but even with these, I would estimate that for my yearly take of grouse I could buy an entire beef cow, cut and wrapped and stored in the meat locker. My checking account balance would be higher if I stayed out of the woods, worked overtime, and ate sirloins.

From our garden we get hundreds of dollars of produce for very little input plus our labor: garlic, squash, lettuce, beans, carrots, radishes, tomatoes, peppers. Some of our food appears in due season like magic, a green fire growing out of the earth with little if any effort on our part: rhubarb, dill, thyme, chives, and quarts of raspberries. Our bees have paid off. When we need cash for our small apiary, we sell pints of honey to recoup the costs. Our firewood goes into the woodshed for the cost of the chainsaw, gas and oil, and, once again, our labor.

All these other endeavors pay, and hunting doesn't, which leads me up against the question: why do I do it? Maybe we hunt because it doesn't compute, because for years we punched the clock, got paid to work for someone else. Grouse and woodcock hunting is work we do for ourselves. We also know what our money buys, and most of what it buys is lacking. Deep down, we know that most of the stuff of this world will end up rotting in a landfill. We know that grouse come dearly, and we are more than happy to pay this steep price.

On the other hand, hunting can and does compute in other ways, just not in cash money. How much is that grouse or woodcock really worth? Look at your smile in the snapshot of you holding a brace of grouse—one brown, one gray. The dog, too, looks tired, but immeasurably happy. I don't look that way when I bring home chicken breasts from Pick 'n Save. I certainly don't have that supermarket feel when I heft a just-shot grouse and smooth back its breast feathers before gently sliding the bird into my game bag.

Fergus eased again into a hard point, his second or third in the last few minutes. I worked my way around him on his right flank, tracing a wide twenty-yard circle and hoping to pin the bird between us. As I made my way back to the dog, I realized it was another ghost point when Fergus had relaxed, dropped his tail, and looked up at me. "Okay," I said when I got alongside him, tapping his head. "No bird." With the tap and those words Fergus was off again on his endless searching. My heart rate and breathing dropped back down near their normal levels. I really thought we had one there.

At that point, we were nearly back to the truck at the end of our hunt, so I worked back out to the trail, my thoughts somewhere other than on the dog. I think I was thinking about the upcoming forecast— the imminent snowstorm that would effectively end the grouse season, burying the rest of the season in a foot of snow. I hadn't had enough hunting, a typical thought this deep into the season, and I didn't want to let autumn go, didn't want to admit that Fergus had finished his eighth season. How many more would we have together?

At some point, I realized I had no idea where the dog was—his bell was silent—and it took me a few moments to spot his white form ten yards off the trail in the popple. I was only thirty yards or so

Gray-phase grouse and Ithaca Ultra Featherlight. (Susan Parman)

from the gate across the trail and my truck on the other side. He was solid, facing toward the trail, but I figured it was probably another ghost point. Besides, I was too close to the truck and too tired to push myself back into the impenetrable popple and blackberry canes. "Fergus, what is it? There's no bird there." He didn't move, so I stood and watched, waiting to see what would happen.

After a half minute, he was still solid as a stone, nose quivering, the long feathering of his tail drifting on a slight current of wind. He wasn't relaxing—if anything it looked as though his intensity was increasing. *Maybe he's got something. Maybe he knows something I don't.* I took two or three steps toward Fergus, and then the blackberry canes edging the trail exploded and up clattered a grouse in my face. I swear I felt the wind its wings made as it passed by, and it seemed to look me in the eye. I flinched backward and nearly dropped my shotgun but got a solid grip on it, threw it to my shoulder, and fired as the bird turned and fled down the trail. The grouse made the mistake of flying in the clear instead of back into the aspen, although a straightaway shot like that is the one I often miss, so you can imagine my surprise when the feathers puffed and the bird tumbled into the grass of the logging road. At that moment, I wouldn't have been surprised if one-hundred-dollar bills started to drop down out of the sky. I felt that lucky, that rich, like I had won the lottery.

Fergus ran up to the bird, mouthed it, left it in the still green grass, then sat next to it politely, as if he was posing for a picture. I picked up the bird and sat down next to him and apologized. "I'm sorry for not believing you, buddy." The grouse was warm and pliant, a big gray-phased bird. A pearl of great price.

What I held warmly in my hands was a great thing for us. I knew this moment sitting side by side on the trail in the shadow of an imminent November snowstorm would come back to me, perhaps years later when Fergus was gone. How much was such a bird worth? Many of us would empty our bank accounts for a moment like this. For something so valuable it would never compute.

Ghost Covert

held the still warm and slack ruffed grouse belly up and admired the stippled breast feathers tinged with blood. Jenkins had jammed his head underneath my arm to get a nose-full of the bird. It was a classical tableau for the bird hunter: the hush of the moment just after the kill—for me, often a moment of regret with the bird in hand. The dog, nudging in for a closer whiff, has none of these regrets.

For years I have been returning to this place, the Ghost Covert, and usually walk the same loop clockwise around it, stopping here at my farthest point north before looping back south to a logging road that runs through a meadow and leads to several more logging roads, which eventually intersect the main gravel road and my parking spot. At this turning point on a ridge above a creek that tumbles over moss-covered boulders the size of suitcases, an old maple tree makes a perfect backrest and provides a view through three mature white pine and across the creek to the north. The trail meanders along this knife-edged ridge, which drops off to the creek on the north and a swampy lake to the south. It's not sublime, like a Rocky Mountain vista, but I can't help sitting here on a sunny October afternoon, watching the maples blaze while munching an apple or a Snickers bar, taking in this quiet beauty.

While Jenkins was burying his nose in the downy breast feathers, I admired the iridescence of its ruff and the grays and chocolates of its fan one last time before tucking it into my game bag. As I stood

Mark follows Fergus and Jenkins into the Ghost Covert, their setter tails waving.
(Susan Parman)

up and was reaching around my back with the bird, I was struck with
a memory from many years before that occurred not ten yards from
where we had paused. Later, I wondered if a particular smell or a
pattern of tree limbs set off the memory. Maybe it was what I had
been eating that triggered it all. Did I also eat an apple that day long
ago? Why I remembered a hunt from fifteen Octobers ago was un-
clear, but it demonstrated how little control I have over my mind
and what flits through there.

That day fifteen years ago I was hunting with Gunnar, a Weimaraner and my first bird dog. We were following up a grouse he

had bumped from down along the creek bottom, and I had labored up the razor-backed ridge from the creek bed trying to keep up with the dog in case we got close to the bird again. If so, I hoped I could control him this time. When we got to the top, he started to make game and shortly was on point just off the trail. He was holding this time. *Ah hah, there it is*, I thought, and just as I started to step toward the dog and with any luck the grouse, a voice behind me croaked, "Hello." I nearly shot myself in the foot. *Shit, another hunter way back in here. He must have walked the trail in from the east as it borders the creek.* Not wanting to miss out on the repointed grouse, I pretended not to hear him and moved in on the bird. I was young and bird crazed and ultimately rude. Just past the dog, a woodcock twittered up—not the grouse I was expecting—and zigzagged along the trail, before it wafted down toward the creek. I didn't fire because I didn't want to miss in front of an audience. Besides, grouse meant a lot more to me than woodcock. I could let woodcock fly away without shooting.

"That was quite a trick," the hunter said when I turned back to him. He had courteously waited on the trail while I flushed the bird. Hearing another voice, Gunnar had popped out of the brushy popple and balsam fir, warily approached the old man, and sniffed the hand he held out, then his pants. I wasn't happy to see this old man, for he was "trespassing" in one of my favorite coverts, but I mustered up a hello.

It's tough for me to say how old he was, but he looked frail, as if he would shatter into a thousand pieces like a pane of glass if he fell off the ridge. He was carrying an old, battered 12 gauge Remington 11-48 and wore thick gray wool pants, the kind made for the cold of deer hunting. With temps in the fifties, it was much too warm for those pants. It had to feel like a sauna inside them, but then maybe he was a crazy old Finn from just down the road where there were Finnish settlements. The old man did have a faint trace of an accent. He didn't have on a vest, just a greasy fanny pack that served as his game bag and perhaps a makeshift belt to hold up his baggy wool pants. He had the look of a wizened old meat hunter. He was probably an old logger.

"What's his name?" He flipped his head in the direction of the dog.

"Gunnar," I answered. The dog had ended his inspection of the old hunter and had moved back into the woods, where I was keeping one eye on him in case he found the grouse and one eye on the old man. "You come in from the east?"

"Yes, yes, I did." I couldn't help staring at his bushy eyebrows, which poked straight out and pointed at me like fingers and ran in a gray continuous line across his forehead. They looked as if they had never been trimmed—virgin eyebrows. I can't recall much of what we said because he wasn't a talker and didn't say much. Besides, I was occupied keeping one eye on the dog in hopes he would contact the grouse we had originally trailed up the ridge.

After a few minutes, the dog did go on point again, and I asked the old man if he would like to join me and flush the bird. He did and I said, "I'll go in the right side of the dog, you take the left." He nodded, and we shouldered our way through the brush over to the dog. When we got up next to Gunnar, I could see he was screwed up tight, usually a sign he was on woodcock. He was a creeper on grouse, always wanting to get closer to a wary and erratic gamebird. I peeked over at the old man as we moved in, and he was white-knuckling his shotgun at port arms, intent on the brush ahead. He looked as though he had done this before.

Before I stepped beyond Gunnar, I spied the woodcock on the ground a few yards in front of the dog. "Woodcock," I said and told the old man I would go in and flush the bird and he could shoot. He nodded again.

The bird got up, twisting through the popple as they will do, and the old man banged away with his semiautomatic. He shot three times and never touched a feather, the bird flushing bat-like over the tops of the trees. Gunnar, meanwhile, had broken at the shot and trailed after the woodcock. I walked down the trail a bit toward the dog and blew my whistle to get him back, and when we returned to the spot of the flush, the old man was gone, slipping back into the dense cover. He had disappeared just as he had arrived—poof, and he was gone. He was in good shape for an old man. Or else I had just seen a ghost.

Heading back, I thought pretty hard about the old man. The rhythmic walking of grouse hunting is good for this. I wondered how the old man snuck up on me like that and then vanished, especially in the dry woods. Over the dry leaves, a squirrel sounded like an elephant. No, that old man was no ghost. He smelled of cigarettes. And I thought I heard him shoot a couple more times before we were out of the woods, a three-shot salute from his old Remington. A ghost would not miss, that much I knew. And a ghost grouse hunter always went afield with a dog, preferably a pointing dog, and a double gun, preferably a side-by-side, as in Corey Ford's story "The Road to Tinkhamtown."

I have seen ghosts here, however. Not Hollywood ghosts or Halloween ghosts, but figments of my imagination layered like page upon page from all the memories and stories of hunting in this place for twenty-five years. It wouldn't surprise me if I met a younger version of myself here. Would I recognize myself? *Who is that young hunter hurrying down the trail?* After all, I have hunted the Ghost Covert more times than any of my other coverts, and I have left a part of myself here. I would hunt this place just for the memories, even if it didn't hold birds, because this place is full of years of my narratives. On the other hand, it has also been pretty reliable at holding birds, and some days here have been truly astonishing.

Just beyond the meadow I mentioned earlier, I ran into the densest concentration of ruffed grouse I've ever seen or ever expect to see. I was hunting that day in 1996 again with Gunnar, and I was carrying what I considered my first real grouse gun—a Savage 330 over-and-under. I fancied the gun because it was made in Finland by Valmet, a country of aspen and grouse. Today, I find it too heavy to lug around the grouse woods. I've been spoiled by age and lighter guns, but on occasion I do like to carry the Valmet and think of former days and hunts. It even reminds me, made as it was in Finland, of that ghost Finlander.

I mention the gun because a grouse actually ran into it that day, flushing from the thick tangle of brush that bordered the swamp I mentioned earlier. (This spot is about two hundred yards from where the old man unleashed his salvo at the woodcock.) If I had been thinking more quickly, I would have batted the bird down as if I was trying to hit a slow curve ball, or hit it like a tennis serve, but instead I was so surprised by a bird boring directly at me that I held the gun up vertically in front of my face in a defensive posture. I thought the bird might veer off at the last moment, but it smashed into the barrels above the hand rest. It careened off my shotgun and kept on flying. Flying into shotgun barrels wasn't any worse than running into saplings and trees, which grouse are wont to do when fleeing, so it was probably fine.

That shotgun I bought used at a pawn shop, and it had been fired often and repeatedly from the looks and feel of it. Thousands of rounds probably went through it before it fell into my hands. It shot loose, the barrels a bit wobbly on the hinge pins, but that wear came in handy in this instance because that old Valmet would fall open like a pickup tailgate. This speeded up reloading since I didn't have to force the gun open as it flopped open of its own accord. I shot as quickly as I could reload.

I would be lying if I had an exact number for how many birds flushed out of the thicket, how many times I shot, and how long all of this took. If I had to guess, at least thirty birds flushed out of this cover the size of a city lot, and I shot twelve to fifteen times, all in a matter of two or three minutes. The only sure thing was the five birds I eventually ended up with, the legal Wisconsin limit.

When I had three birds on the ground, I decided I needed to stop shooting and collect them before I lost one, even though birds continued to flush. Gunnar, always a good retriever, had plunged after the downed birds, which flushed even more birds, so I shot two more and hoped we would find them all. I'm surprised we ever recovered all the birds. I went after the last two, which had flushed away from the swamp into an older popple/oak stand that wasn't as brushy as the thicket where the birds were holed up. I figured it would be easiest for me to find those in the more open cover, while Gunnar rooted around in the brush for the others. Even as we both searched for all the dead birds, he put up more birds. If another hunter with decent shooting skills had been with me that day, I have no doubt we would have killed ten birds, a double limit. I've never seen concentrated bird numbers like that, except while duck hunting. I don't expect to ever see such a multitude of grouse like that again, except in my dreams.

The five birds almost didn't fit in my vest. But I got them jammed in and started the long walk out of the woods with the weight of five grouse tugging down my shoulders and the birds warming my back as though I were wearing a heating pad. I stopped every so often and took off my vest and recounted the birds to make sure one hadn't fallen out. Once we got back to the truck, I pulled them all out and lined them up on the trail, and Gunnar went down the line smelling each one. I had to make sure they were real, not simply figments of my imagination.

I have worked through this cover dozens of times since that improbable day and all those flushes and birds. Since then, I haven't put up more than a couple of birds at a time, never that overwhelming number from what now seems an unrecognizable life. The older I get, the more unreal that day seems—as if those five birds riding snuggly against my back were merely apparitions. Or ghosts.

Jesus Covert

When I saw the camo bible resting on the dusty dash of the Ford pickup, as though it were perched on a church altar, I did a double take. *Jeez, is that a camo bible?* I had to come back for one more look after walking away, just to make sure my eyes weren't deceiving me. It was as if I had seen an albino deer or a two-headed turkey.

The pickup was parked in a pull-off where we had planned to start our hunt, and I had jumped out to see if the owners were grouse hunting. Empty boxes of small-shot shells, blaze-orange hats and vests, dog collars, and kennels are the tools of grouse and woodcock hunters. If they were bird hunting, I would drive down the road to find some other place to hunt—we had plenty of other coverts in the area. The Ford's owner was bow hunting deer, so I parked, got out, and gathered my gear.

We had a noticeably quiet hunt and didn't shoot a single bird, not even a woodcock—apparently I or the cover hadn't been blessed that day. From a bird's point of view, however, it had been a blessed day. I wondered if the guy with the camo bible had been graced with a deer. I would have asked him about that, but his truck was gone when we got back to the pull-off. Lately, I had been missing a lot of birds, even some gimme shots—maybe I needed to spend more of my Sundays in church rather than out in the woods attending grouse church. Start tithing my hunting time. Or maybe order a camo bible.

At any rate, the camo bible intrigued me. Later that afternoon back at home, I pulled up amazon.com. Sure enough there it was, in multiple versions and camo patterns for Christian hunters, including pink camo for the huntress in the family. Morbidly curious, I scrolled through several versions and read the blurbs, like this one:

> The perfect gift for Father's Day, a son's birthday, graduation, or any time, The Sportsman's Bible is ideal to slip into a pocket and carry into the field. The Mothwing™ fall mimicry camouflage pattern cover and darkened page edges are non-reflective and won't scare game. In addition to the full text of the Holman Christian Standard Bible® translation, The Sportsman's Bible contains numerous devotions written for hunters and fishermen that connect the timeless principles of God's Word with the passion of millions of North American outdoors enthusiasts. In 2000, over fifteen million Americans purchased hunting licenses, and thirty million bought fishing licenses. Churches are becoming aware of this significant market and are sponsoring wild game dinners and father-son ministries that focus on men's interest in hunting and fishing. Jason Cruise, founder of the Tennessee Outdoor Network and Coordinator of Outdoor Ministries for the Tennessee Baptist Convention, is executive editor of the special devotional section which includes articles by well-known sportsmen plus helpful outdoors tips ("Setting Up a Ground Blind," "Tree Stand Safety," "The Hunter's Code," etc.).

Obviously, this sort of bible was not meant for mother, daughter, or girlfriend, but I digress. Camo has lately become fashionable in our culture, particularly in the Midwest, where some Christians feel comfortable enough to wear it to church, so I suppose a camo bible decked out in Mossy Oak Break-Up or Realtree Hardwoods was inevitable. I shouldn't have been surprised.

Cabela's retails camo furniture and camo curtains to dress up the home; we can order camo pajamas or camo lingerie. It is no longer the signature of poor college students or homeless Vietnam vets.

One of the blurbs for another camo bible claimed its "fashionable camo design makes it fun to carry your Bible wherever you go." A fun bible. Many people get sucked in by Amazon ads and jacket blurbs—who hasn't?—becoming, as the ad copy stated, a "significant market." Not people or Christians, but a "market" waiting to be tapped. Bible consumers.

Many churchgoers around here hunt. They're down-to-earth people who feel persecuted by the godless, liberal elites of the East and West Coasts. I get the collusion of outdoor enthusiast and Christian values. Much of my surprise stems from my upbringing in a fundamentalist Baptist church in the seventies, where camo was decidedly not fashionable, especially for church clothes, and definitely not for a bible. Back then, the guys who wore camo (Old School, the only pattern available, usually from the local surplus store) were those *skipping* church on Sunday morning to go hunting or fishing. They smoked cigarettes, drank beer, and belched in public. They swore a lot and drove old rusty pickups. If they attended church at all, it was Mass on Saturday afternoon, what we called "fishing Mass," which wouldn't interfere much with catching crappies or bullheads.

A couple of my friends had dads like those, and I was thrilled when invited to tag along on their hunting or fishing expeditions, say, out to Lake Meyer for bluegills or maybe some roadside pheasant hunting late in the season. One of my friend's dads could swear as though he had worked as a deckhand on a Mississippi barge, turning the air blue like the cigarette smoke drifting around the Friendly Tap, where I collected for the newspaper I delivered to its door every morning. When my buddy or I tried out a swear word or two in front of his dad, he exploded. "Goddammit, I told you little bastards to stop cussing. Jesus Christ, suppose your mother heard. Damn," his dad hollered. Those illicit words just seemed a natural match to the excitement of road hunting as we bounced around in the backseat of his dad's Ford Falcon, scanning the ditches and fields for roosters.

I did absorb a smattering of theology in the string of Baptist churches we attended. On occasion I did listen, between the many hours I sat on a hard pew dreaming I was somewhere else, like fishing or hunting. On Sundays in the fall, I spent the time between our church's morning and evening services, a precious few hours of glorious October or November, roaming the fields with either my .22 or my 12 gauge, depending on the game I hoped to flush. It didn't seem like the bible, at least the version I had (leather-bound NIV), was big on hunting. In fact, the bible presented me with a theological conundrum because, if anything, its pages seemed ambivalent about hunting.

There was Nimrod, who was the "first on earth to become a mighty man" (Genesis 10:8) and who was also "a mighty hunter before the LORD" (Genesis 10:9). Jehovah favored this man. Later in Genesis, chapter 27, is the story of Jacob and Esau. When their father, Isaac, was on his death bed, he instructed Esau to gather his weapons, go out into the field, and kill some beast so he could have one last meal of wild game. After this feast, Isaac would bless his older son, the hunter. Jacob, Esau's younger brother, who was domestic and devious, fooled Isaac—while Esau was out hunting for this meat—into thinking he was Esau by dressing in hairy garments.

Falling for this ruse, the old man gave his blessing to Jacob, instead of Esau, the rightful heir. Jacob swindled both his father and his older brother. We can read this story as the triumph of the settled life of the farmer over the wild and nomadic life of the hunter, as Israel was a nation looking for its promised land so it could end its years wandering in the wilderness. However you read the story, the hunter got double-crossed.

In the New Testament, the character of Jesus is entirely different from the Old Testament God. He defended the weak, the poor, the politically oppressed, women, and children. He fed people with bread and fish; he made wine for a wedding. He possessed supernatural sensitivity. "Are not two sparrows sold for a penny? And not one of them will fall to the ground without your Father's will. But even the hairs of your head are numbered. Fear not, therefore; you are of more value than many sparrows" (Matthew 10:31–33). Jesus's sensitivity and charity toward life are clear in Matthew's gospel.

For this reason, I can't imagine Jesus in camo because of the violence and militarism it suggests. Instead, I can picture him with a fishing rod in his hand. His first two disciples, brothers Peter and Andrew, were fishing when Jesus called them. "Follow me and I will make you fishers of men" (Matthew 4:19). The next two disciples, brothers James and John, were mending nets out in their boat when Jesus called them. Jesus miraculously created fish when he fed the five thousand—no catch and release that day. After Jesus was crucified, Peter was miserably depressed so he decided to go fishing and convinced several disciples to go along with him. They fished through the night and caught nothing. In the morning Jesus appeared and told them to cast their net on the right side of the boat. "So they cast it, and now they were not able to haul it in, for the quantity of fish" (John 21:6). So I could see the point of a fishing bible, with a water-proof Gore-Tex cover.

The next time I hunted the Jesus Covert (quicker and easier to say than the Camo Bible Covert), the pull-off was empty. Fergus and I had the place to ourselves on a Sunday—grouse church for us. We didn't put up many birds that early November day, but in one of the birdier corners, I nearly stepped on a grouse loafing in the grass of an old logging road. Fergus was off to my left working a promising aspen cutting and missed the one underfoot, as is often the case. I'm always so stunned when a bird gets up at my feet. Then again, they were native to this place, having grown up here like the aspen or the balsam fir. Their lives were knit together with this place.

Despite my jangled nerves, I recovered and got my shotgun to my shoulder as the bird flushed straight down the logging road and bulldozed through the aspen cutting. It was rising slightly, about as easy a shot a grouse hunter gets in the woods. When I had covered the bird, I pulled the trigger—once, twice, a third time. Nothing happened—I had jammed the safety on my Browning between the barrel selectors—and the grouse flew away unharmed. Maybe I needed to give the Jesus Covert a rest for a while.

We didn't get another shot until the end of the day when we were almost back to the pull-off. By then, I was thinking I sorely needed to buy a camo bible. It couldn't hurt, I figured. On a whim, I decided at the last moment to hunt a little side cover, and almost immediately into this cover Fergus hit on a hard point. I got around Fergus and put the bird up, but as it hammered through the thick cover, I didn't get a shot at it until it popped out in the clear above the trees at least thirty yards away. I threw an end-of-the-day desperation shot at it, and the bird remarkably tumbled. Was I surprised—a gift bird. Fergus raced away at the shot.

I marked it well, as it was, for me, a long shot in the grouse woods, but I needn't have worried about recovering it, as I found Fergus nosing it dead on the ground. This bird was satisfying in manifold ways. A bird at the end of the day as the sun is setting is always an unforeseen blessing. That late in the day, I had already given up and accepted the notion of going home empty-handed. This gift, plus the good dog work and for once some good shooting on my part, was much more than I deserved.

The bird in hand was heaven sent, and so was Fergus, sitting and panting by my side and the creation—the lovely northern woods—surrounding us. This message of gratitude, so clear even a fool like me can read it, lies between the covers of every bible, even a camo one.

New Wood

Among Wolves

In late June 2015, a friend of a friend was walking his two black Labs on trails in the Bayfield County Forest, just a few miles south of Cable, Wisconsin, where he lives. He had taken this walk many times. He knew about wolves, that a pack roamed the area's woodland. Suddenly his younger Lab charged up over a ridge and out of sight, and he heard an odd noise shortly thereafter. About forty-five minutes later, his older Lab found its kennel mate down in a heavily wooded pothole, lying on its side, looking as if it were taking a nap. The dog died of a broken back, the wolves having grabbed the dog and pulled in opposite directions, severing the spinal cord.

Hearing this anecdote has fueled a recurring nightmare for me—the dog (usually Fergus) works too far away, out of sight and earshot beyond a far ridge, despite my frantic whistling and yelling. When I finally reach what's left of him, down in some creek bed, he's been stripped of all his flesh except his head and a single forelock. My living and breathing setter in just a few seconds has been rendered into a stark, white skeleton, while I flutter about the woods terrified and helpless, fully conscious of what has happened to my dog. I started having these nightmares several years ago after a friend showed me a picture of a wolf-killed bear hound. Except for its head and one front paw, the wolves had stripped the hound's flesh to the bone. The wolves ran down, killed, and then devoured this bear hound in the midst of New Wood, one of my favorite grouse and woodcock covers. Making matters worse, the same pack attacked and injured an English setter here the day after Christmas in 2015.

Twenty years ago, I didn't have these nightmares because so few wolves roamed northern Wisconsin and posed little danger. They were fictional beasts we heard about every now and then—rumors and phantoms. Today, however, they roam the northern half of the state and inhabit every covert I hunt. Their numbers have greatly exceeded the Endangered Species Act target number of 350, and a hunting and trapping season was instituted and held for three years from 2012 to 2014. In December 2014, when the Humane Society of the United States won a decision in federal court, the wolf was relisted as an endangered species in the Midwest, and the U.S. Court of Appeals for the District of Columbia upheld this decision on August 1, 2017. The hunting/trapping season was suspended, so their numbers continue to climb. The 2016–17 winter count estimated that 925 wolves in 232 packs roamed Wisconsin, a 16 percent increase over the previous year's wolf count. The Wisconsin DNR continues to work at delisting the wolf so it can be managed at the state rather than the federal level.

One hundred years ago, we had nearly annihilated wolves in Wisconsin, *Canis lupis* having been relentlessly hounded by government bounties and the public's wrath and paranoia. Richard Thiel, in his book *The Timber Wolf in Wisconsin*, writes of the celebrated death of infamous Old Two Toes in Bayfield County in 1959, the last high-profile wolf death in the state. After that, there were fleet sightings and rumors, but few if any wolves were left in the state. Then in 1975, a vehicle struck and killed a wolf south of Superior on Highway 35, and Wisconsin DNR officials were surprised to confirm the unexpected death of a yearling female, the first confirmed killing of a wolf in the state since Old Two Toes. Four years later, another wolf was struck and killed by a car, this time on a gravel road in the New Wood area, in the north-central part of the state. New Wood is in western Lincoln County and 130 miles from the Minnesota border from whence the wolves were thought to be infiltrating Wisconsin. New Wood has a history with wolves.

As do I. In all my years of grouse hunting, all my hours in the woods, I have glimpsed only one wolf, this over ten years ago. It was running through a stand of mature popple in a county forest. At first, I saw a big body and immediately thought deer, and then I recognized a canine and thought coyote. But when I saw a thick collar around its neck, I whistled for the dog, collared him, and hustled off in the opposite direction. I knew it was a wolf.

I have once been within spitting distance of a wolf, this time as I was riding my bicycle through the county forest on a gravel road that bisects the 6,400 acres. There is only one sharp corner on this road, and as I rounded it, I nearly crashed into the side of a lanky black wolf standing broadside in the road. I slammed on the brakes, skidded toward the wolf, and yelled, "Holy shit!" The wolf was as surprised as I was. He jumped, all four legs in the air, and took off running, legs churning before he hit the gravel of the road. He beelined for the trees, and the woods swallowed him instantly. Had I the wolf's olfactory power, I could have smelled it before I nearly smashed into it. I wheeled around back to where my skid marks were on the gravel road and peered into the dark woods. It dawned on me that maybe there were others, maybe an entire pack, so I quickly pedaled away, my heart pounding in my ears.

The previous year, I was motorcycling on a lonely stretch of Highway 70 in Price County and topped out over a low rise on the highway. Down below in a shallow valley, I spotted four-legged movement and thought deer. As I shifted down and rolled up closer, I could see that it was a canine. It was a wolf, dining on a road-killed deer, and as I approached, it was reluctant to leave the carcass. Lifting its head from the putrid flesh, it displayed a muzzle smeared with blood and gore. It stared at me, a little too long for my comfort, before it loped down into the ditch. It turned around before it made the tree line and stared at me, as I squeezed by in the far right side of the lane. Even though I was astride a five-hundred-pound machine, I was the one intimidated, and I can still see that bloody muzzle and the penetrating eyes. It was not an image of the cute little wolf dog, the image ironed onto thousands of T-shirts and sweatshirts and sold to tourists visiting northern Wisconsin resort towns.

Wolves roam in virtually every covert I hunt. Even though I've had less than a half-dozen wolf sightings in a couple of decades, seeing their spoor is a common occurrence, nearly an everyday event in most of my coverts. I find their steel-wool scat lying on many of the trails I hunt, a reminder of their presence. Sometimes these scats are left so blatantly obvious, it seems they're advertisements. In winter, particularly when the snow is deep and they take to the packed snow of trails, their large tracks and urine markings are clear signs of their passing, their ceaseless movement. I catch myself stopping now and then in some out-of-the-way place in the woods and looking around, keenly feeling that wolves are somewhere in the brush and trees just out of my sight, silently watching me. It's an ancient, unfounded fear fueling my nightmares.

The nursery tales we heard or had read to us as children—Little Red Riding Hood, the Three Little Pigs—have stoked our fears of wolves and contributed to the creation of the myth of the Big Bad Wolf. My nightmares, like the popular notion that wolves prey on humans, particularly small children, are based on irrational fears, not science. They do on occasion prey on livestock and dogs; however, a wolf killing an upland dog is a rare occurrence in the Upper Midwest. In truth, our bird dogs are much more likely to be mowed down by a speeding vehicle or laid low by tick-borne diseases or blastomycosis. We are more likely to cause their deaths. I know of one local hunter who shot and killed his best friend's dog while hunting pheasants. Dogs can overheat and die in the field, as dozens did years ago when, on opening day of the pheasant season, temps soared into the nineties in South Dakota. Even the slow and seemingly dim-witted porcupine can be deadly, the infected quills occasionally killing dogs. I really should have Lyme disease or porcupine nightmares if I thought rationally in REM sleep mode.

I know these facts—and yet. In 2015, according to the Wisconsin DNR, wolves killed twenty-two dogs in Wisconsin, the majority bear hounds that course unattended through some of the wildest areas of the state. They also advertise their trespassing through wolf territory with their constant baying. Several other types of dogs were injured, including two English setters, although comparing bear hound victims to bird dog victims gives me some hope, since upland hunters keep much closer contact with their dogs while hunting. This close human presence deters wolves.

My setters would be no match for wolves should they unfortunately encounter them while hunting. Wolves are bigger, stronger, and faster, their teeth, claws, and genes honed by wilderness. Dogs, like humans, have lost their edge for survival in a natural but hostile environment. Fergus, I hope, might be able to fend for himself until I arrived on the scene, but Jenkins would be no match for wolves. They are both lovers, not fighters, nothing like the uberdog Buck in *Call of the Wild*, who dominated the arctic wilds. Their vulnerability, and the risk to which I'm subjecting them while hunting, forces me to confront the reality of putting a mostly helpless setter down in wolf country.

Like ticks bearing Lyme disease or the Powassan virus, wolves make their home in northern Wisconsin—and if I want to grouse hunt, I must accept the risk of hunting among them with my setters. They come with the territory.

Paradise Lost

In twenty-five years of grouse hunting, I have run out of shells just twice, and both times were in spots where friends had taken me. I was a guest in their covert. This speaks to either the generosity of my friends or my inability at finding good cover.

Or not bringing along enough shells. When grouse hunting, I'm not at all routine when it comes to filling up my pockets with shells. I never count out a specific number nor do I dump a full box of shells in each pocket, like a friend who stuffs them in like acorns in a chipmunk's cheeks. Instead, I grab a handful of $7\frac{1}{2}$s or 8s and drop them into one pocket and then drop a handful of 9s into the other pocket. Some days I grab whatever shells I have left behind the seat of my truck.

On most hunts, I typically end up carrying fifteen shells, give or take a few. When it comes to grouse shooting, I'm a realist, not an optimist. On hunts too numerous to count, I have dropped a pair of shells in my over-and-under at the beginning of the day, only to pull out those same two unspent shells at the end of the day. Those days, I feel like throwing a beer can (plenty in our Wisconsin ditches) in the air and peppering it, just so I can feel as if I've accomplished something.

At any rate, I ran out of shells in both places because they were thick with grouse, and I shot until my barrels were hot and my pockets empty. Fifteen shells and the Wisconsin limit is five birds per day—you do the math. Part of the problem is that shots on grouse are typically scarce, even in a place like northern Wisconsin, and this can lend itself to sloppy shooting—a lot of unnecessary and wasteful shots we shouldn't take—and it's the reason I don't shoot an auto-loader and stuff it full of five shells. When you're down to your last two shells, you tend to regret all your wasted shots, that fifty-yard crosser, the one going away that was a mere speck on the horizon when you pulled the trigger. I suppose this begs the obvious question of why I don't carry more shells. It has something to do with weight, or maybe I'm subconsciously trying to train myself to take better shots.

Pete showed me the first cover, a tag alder swamp bordering a busy state highway. It always made me nervous to work my dogs there with the constant stream of cars, pickups, and semis whistling by. I would plant myself between the dog and the highway and never let him cross my path and get within fifty yards of the highway, even if he was working a bird that direction. Susan had more than once told me the story of her ancient and deaf Viszla who was crushed by a semi on a state highway when she was in middle school, and that story was always in my mind when I hunted here. No number of ruffed grouse was worth a dead setter.

It also didn't feel like grouse hunting, with all the highway noise. You could hear the steel belts of radial tires slapping down the concrete for miles and miles. But there were scores of birds in those monkey trees, so I risked the safety of my dogs and told myself to forget aesthetics. Those tag alders were hell to fight through, but with all the flushes, it was nirvana.

Together Pete and I shot three or four ruffed grouse that day, which took all our ammo, at least thirty shots. We left several dozen birds in that tag alder jungle, so I came back alone a few weeks later, this time with a full box of shells. I figured since Pete's covert was right along the highway, it was fair game, even though in the arcane rules of grouse hunting it was technically his. He also hunted with a standard poodle, surely a forfeiture releasing his ownership rights to the place. Besides, any experienced grouse hunter cruising by on the highway would intuitively know this was good cover and could stop and legally hunt it. It was public land along a state highway—this cover was no secret—so I figured Pete wouldn't mind. Better I hunt here than some stranger, I rationalized.

For three productive years I hunted this cover, referring to it as the Honey Hole. I was surprised it continued to hold so many birds despite being situated in plain sight right off a state highway. I shot a lot of birds in those tag alders, until one October—my first visit there that grouse season—I pulled into the lot, turned off the engine, and stared out the windshield. The county had leveled the tag alders, clear-cutting the entire cover. It was farewell to these once happy woods. I was so stunned by the destruction I didn't even hunt that day, even though there were thousands of other acres of public land in the immediate area. I turned around and drove home, confusing the dog. *Had my greed, my gluttony for ruffed grouse, doomed this sweet land?*

Ten years later, it still hasn't grown back thick, like when we first hunted it. Today it looks more like a prairie. An old-timer told me he used to hunt sharp-tailed grouse here, so maybe it has reverted to its original state. I checked on it dutifully for several seasons every September, hoping the tags would grow back, but eventually gave up and crossed it off my list. Maybe the land managers thought popple would replace the gnarly old tag alders, as it did across the road when they cut the old tag alders on that side, but not much of anything has grown back. The county foresters sure made a hell of that heaven.

A bureaucratic decision razed this first grouse heaven, but the second, I simply lost. Technically I didn't lose it; I could just never find my way back there after I had tasted its sweetness.

Another friend guided me to the second covert—after a couple of false starts earlier in the morning. Ross and I, if we're honest, were a bit competitive about our grouse hunting at this time twenty years ago. We were both young, athletic, and keen on grouse hunting. For that reason, we were fairly tight-lipped about our coverts, not wanting to divulge our secrets. We once surprised each other, meeting deep in a covert each of us thought was "ours." We had a good laugh over that one.

Since Ross was driving that morning, I left it up to him to determine where we would hunt. He would have to take me to some of "his" spots. Despite not owning a deed, we felt as if we owned our coverts, had exclusive rights there. Trespassing on each other's ground was against our unwritten rules, but even so we didn't want to reveal too much about our spots. I figured he was taking me to a second-best place, since that's what I would have done if I were in his shoes.

As we rolled down a logging road to the first pull-off of the day, a grouse darted across the road and cartwheeled off the bumper. Ross slammed on the brakes, and we jumped out to look for the bird, which had tumbled in a puff of feathers into the ditch on my side of the road. "We find this bird, you're counting it against your limit," I joked, although much truth is said in jest. For sure, I wasn't going to claim it against the five birds I planned on shooting that day. We found it shortly, a mass of bloody feathers and broken bones, and left it in the ditch. We left it for a coyote, a fox, perhaps a crow. The dogs were whining in their crates, impatient to start the day.

We continued on down the logging road, only to find a truck parked there. Dog kennels in the box and Kentucky plates. We groused about out-of-state hunters as we turned around and headed back out to the county highway and someplace else. I probably said something like, "It's getting to be like Park Falls down here." (Park Falls, Wisconsin, markets itself as the Ruffed Grouse Capital of the World, and thus attracts scads of out-of-state hunters.)

After driving a few more miles north, toward Medford, we pulled off a gravel road in the county forest. Ross said he wanted to check out a new covert, which is something I would have done if I were him—take your hunting partner to a place you've always wondered about but never hunted. Many of these spots don't pan out, and you can check them off your list. I had brought along my setter, Ox, and Ross had his two setters, Duke and Sadie. It was a family affair, as Duke was Ox's uncle, Sadie his half sister.

Ross put down Sadie, I got Ox out, and we started up each side of a tag alder–lined creek. The creek meandered through an older popple cutting, most of the aspen well past their prime. These trees looked anywhere from twenty to thirty years old. I had my doubts about this place, but as I was essentially the guest, I kept my thoughts to myself. We put up a couple of grouse, and one of us may have taken a shot, but we returned to the truck after a couple of hours, empty-handed.

We ate a sandwich, and I swigged coffee out of my thermos as Ross checked one of the many maps stashed behind the front seat. "I think we should go check this place out," he said, pointing to a spot on his map a few miles north and west of us. I said OK, not really paying much attention. Nor did I pay much attention on the drive over there. Badger football was on the radio (Ross attended the UW and I worked for a branch of the UW), and I was tuned in to the game and not really watching where we were going.

At the next stop, we geared up with all the doors open and the radio on. Today I can't even remember who Wisconsin was playing or why this football game was so important. Ross wanted to work both his dogs, and there was no way Ox was going to be left behind, so we set off with all three setters. As we started in on the cover, I wasn't confident about this place either since it looked a lot like the spot we had hunted earlier in the morning—tag alders mixed among mature popple.

We trudged around for an hour, perhaps longer, with little luck, but we kept going deeper into the woods, exploring new territory.

Ross's business partner, also a grouse hunter, had his pilot's license, and they had flown over this area in summer looking for clear-cuts. Ross was determined we would run into hot cover if we kept going deeper in the woods. "Just one more ridge," Ross kept saying. "Let's see what's beyond that tree line."

Then beyond the next tree line, we started to hit birds, both grouse and woodcock. They came fast and furious. At one time, we had all three dogs on point on three different birds. Figuring out which dog to go to first wasn't a bad dilemma to have. It was a beautiful thing to see three setters related by blood all on point at the same time.

We started to shoot birds, and the dogs kept pointing as we tried to collect the birds and keep up with the dogs, who kept drawing us farther and farther away from our starting point, deeper and deeper into the woods. But we didn't care—we would have walked all the way to Lake Superior for this.

At some point, one of us mentioned the Double Double, a double limit of both grouse and woodcock, and at that time, the midnineties, five woodcock was the daily limit in Wisconsin. It has since been lowered to a more sensible three per day. So ten grouse and ten woodcock between the two of us. I don't know how we would even have carried such a bloody haul out of the woods, and writing this twenty years later, I'm struck by both my intensity and my gluttony. But such is youth.

At some point, however, we woke out of our reverie and noticed the sun sinking toward the tops of the trees in the West. It was time to find our way out of the woods if we didn't want to camp out under the stars with just the dogs as blankets. Besides, I was down to my last shell and realized the Double Double wasn't to be.

We took a bearing due west on the tallest white pine and made off in that direction, now annoyed at the dogs, who continued to point woodcock. I wouldn't say we were panicking, but we had no idea how far away the road lay or, to be honest, in which direction it was, and the woods were quickly darkening. We figured it was west and went that way.

In the end, we did cut a road a bit after the sun set, turned right on the gravel, and started down it toward where we thought we had parked. Of course, this could have been any gravel road, but what choice did we have except to follow it? I hadn't been paying much attention to my compass all afternoon as we hunted our way deeper into the woods. I was trusting Ross. GPS would have solved this predicament, but it was years away. Besides, what fun would that have been?

Eventually, we made it back, using the tiny bit of feeble light in the West. I could still see my feet as we trudged down the road, although we were almost on top of the truck before we could make out its bulk looming on the shoulder. We pulled out our birds and piled them on the tailgate—five grouse and six woodcock. It was too dark for a tailgate shot, not that either of us had a camera on us at the time. Cell phones with cameras were also years away in the future.

In the light of the pickup's cab, I looked at my lanyard counter—it read fifty-six. We had flushed fifty-six grouse that day (I was counting all flushes, including possible reflushes). This still stands as the most grouse I had ever put up in one day. Grouse numbers were higher back then, the peaks of each succeeding grouse cycle since the midnineties lower than the previous high, so, at the time, I didn't really understand how remarkable this day was. I was young with years of grouse hunting ahead of me—no doubt I thought I would see those big numbers again someday. Besides, I was hungry, thirsty, and dog tired. I would have traded my grouse for a cold Mountain Dew. My kingdom for an icy beer.

When I got home, Susan was watching the ten o'clock news, worried she would see a story about a pickup flipped upside down in the ditch or one about a hunting accident, some moron shooting his buddy in the back: "I thought he was a grouse." Or she figured we had more likely stopped off at a roadside bar, and don't think we weren't tempted by the many country dives we passed driving home. Instead, we settled for the first convenience store.

I hadn't been paying attention on the drive in or on the drive out, when it was dark and I was fatigued and hungry. The next day, I didn't even remember off what road we had hunted. I wasn't even sure what county we were in. Furthermore, this was Ross's spot—he had sniffed it out—so I stayed away. Besides, there were plenty of grouse in plenty of other places.

As the years passed, however, my myth of that day grew, particularly in the trough of the following grouse cycle when birds were scarce. I took to calling this place Paradise. When the hunting was at its rock-bottom worst, whenever I found myself driving around Taylor County, I wondered where Paradise lay. In those years of low bird numbers, I figured I could shoot just as many birds driving around on logging roads as I could humping it through the woods, and my dogs have all loved riding around in a truck. I don't know what I was looking for—Eden Road, Nirvana, Oz, a billboard advertising Heaven's Acres. Maybe we would run into the angel Uriel guarding the flaming gates to Paradise.

Twice over the years, I got out and explored areas that looked as though they might lead to Paradise, but each time I came home birdless and baffled as to where that long-gone place was. Both these potential coverts had matured beyond their best bird-producing primes, both were silent and gray, and honestly, after stomping around for a while, I wasn't sure I was in the right area. Neither place looked right, and I left the wild woods forlorn.

It took years for me to realize that in the context of grouse and woodcock hunting, Paradise is a fleeting notion. It's inevitable: Each and every one of our grouse heavens will one day mature and die off—and come to an end, no matter how much we want things to remain the same. And then all we have left are the myths, our memories, and our stories. I can now live with that.

Somewhere in Clark County

"Point. I gotta point over here," I yelled back over my shoulder. Fergus had pinned a grouse somewhere just ahead in the screen of young aspen and tangle of brush. I stood on a faint trail behind the dog, hoping the two Daves would find us quickly so we could move in, flush the bird, and with any luck capture this moment on film, which was why we were here. I was hunting with Dave Carlson in Clark County, Wisconsin, and we were filming a grouse/woodcock episode for his outdoor TV show, *Northland Adventures*. The other Dave was the cameraman, heroically lugging a hefty twenty-pound professional camera through the dense cover.

After waiting impatiently a half minute or so, I yelled again, this time as loud as I could. Locked up on the scent, Fergus's sides and flews heaved as he drank in the heavy bird scent. *What's taking them so long? How long can he hold this point?* White-knuckling my shotgun, I was coiled up, ready to swing on a rising bird. A few seconds after my second hail, the bird burst out of the brush, perhaps unnerved by my yelling. I shot it before it got up out of the popples, a relatively easy shot of fifteen to twenty yards through the brush. It fell on my first shot, and Fergus dove headlong into the brush after it.

It was textbook grouse hunting, all except the standing there and waiting for the camera. It was picture perfect as well—apart from not getting the picture. I had the grouse in hand, the dog nosing it, when the Daves finally arrived, the best part of the narrative unrecorded.

Flush counter: a good day in the woods. (Susan Parman)

Although we did film a couple of woodcock points and shots, this was the only grouse we got close to that day. The episode aired a few weeks later, and that moment—the grouse point, the flush, and the shot, even the autumn blue of the October sky—was reduced to my holding the bird in my hand and pointing out its subtle features to all those tuned in on Sunday morning: the gray tail feathers, the dark, oil-colored ruff, the mottled breast feathers. The digital version was a poor substitute for what we experienced in the field that day. Not only did virtual reality miss the dog's point, the grouse flushing, the shot, the bird falling, it missed so much of the intensity of that particular moment, or for that matter, an October day of grouse hunting in the woods.

On the other hand, for some TV viewers that episode may have been their introduction to upland hunting, their only window to a grouse hunt. Perhaps the show set some kid to dreaming about his first shotgun or his first bird dog. Or maybe a grouse hunter too old and broken down to hunt was watching that morning. There was some consolation in reaching this audience.

But for those of us who know the real thing, the virtual doesn't begin to compare with the most ordinary grouse hunt. Sometime in the future when Fergus is dead and gone, I might pull out my DVD copy and revisit that October day and be thankful that at least I have a digital representation of him. But I wouldn't trade a hundred hours of him on film for an hour of following him through the woods.

We live in a world saturated with media of all kinds, and children today grow up with this 24/7 screen saturation. According to a 2015 Common Sense in Media report, teens in the United States spend about nine hours per day using media for their enjoyment. These nine hours, longer than the average workday or time spent sleeping, include time watching TV, videos, and movies; playing video games; reading online; listening to music; and checking social media. Furthermore, a 2012 Canadian survey (David Suzuki Foundation) claimed that 70 percent of thirteen- to twenty-year-olds stated they spent an hour or less outside each day, and most of that hour was used up in pedestrian transportation—like walking or biking to school or a friend's house—and not in exploring nature. No wonder researchers and journalists have referred to this generation as "screenagers." Lest those of us who are older think we're immune to technology, we are just as susceptible to screen addiction.

Regardless of the media, it always mediated the experience between the audience and the subject at hand. We forget this is the meaning of media. It is the glass through which we look, shaping and coloring our experiences, often without our knowledge, let alone consent. This occurs in our oldest of mediums—the five hundred years of print since Gutenberg. When I write, it is I as author who mediates the experience for the reader, who filters and manages the narrative and the information. This is an enormous responsibility, getting things right and true, which is one of the reasons the author signs her or his name to the document. This accountability isn't as clear in other media, particularly on screen.

In our highly mediated age, we experience fewer and fewer things directly. One of the reasons I hunt is that the grocery store mediates the experience of eating meat, or eating fruits and vegetables for that matter. When I buy shrink-wrapped chicken breasts from my local supermarket, I don't know where the bird came from, what it ate, how it lived, how it was treated. I have no idea how it was "processed." Chicken McNuggets are perhaps the most mediated meal we can buy, the chicken in the product almost unrecognizably mediated until we don't even realize we're eating a once living and breathing being.

More and more of our lives are mediated. Our cars mediate landscape. We look out the window as the land flows by at seventy miles per hour. We can't smell the flowers in the ditches or hear the bees buzzing around as they pollinate the blossoms. We don't experience the weather in our climate-controlled interiors—the temperature, the humidity, the wind. We can't appreciate the texture of the ground or the pull of gravity as we ascend a grade. How different I experience the landscape when I walk through it hunting.

I always wonder what my dogs think with the landscape whizzing by outside the windshield. They get a much better sense of the world with the windows rolled down and their noses out in the slipstream. With their noses, they can read and understand the world. My dogs love to do this, as most dogs do. My dogs, happily for them, do not understand TV, the one-dimensional screen. Occasionally, they cock their ears at a bark on TV, but in general it means nothing to them. Once again we are reminded how we should live our lives and experience the world much more like dogs.

Compared with the overwhelming number of videos about deer, turkey, elk, and duck hunting for sale or on the internet, relatively few grouse- and woodcock-hunting videos are available, but with the prevalence of smartphones and GoPros more upland hunting gets filmed each season. Grouse and woodcock hunting is hard to film, or film well, given the dense cover these birds prefer and their erratic flush rates. At times, it's like filming in a telephone booth or a closet, but in the last few years, I've seen some interesting grouse and woodcock video, most of it short, amateur stuff.

Pheasant, chukar, or sharp-tailed hunting, with the open expanses of their western habitat, provides a much more manageable environment and backdrop for film. Hunting preserves and planted birds would make for even easier filming, and no doubt a significant amount of upland bird hunting gets filmed on game preserves, but we have no game farms for ruffed grouse and woodcock. They live only in wild and sometimes unmanageable landscape. In one sense, it's a good thing very little grouse or woodcock hunting gets filmed.

People have been filming hunting since the invention of the movie camera. When TV sets appeared in American homes in the fifties, hunting shows soon followed. As a kid, I frequently tuned in to *The American Sportsman* hosted by Curt Gowdy. I can still remember the episodes when Captain Kirk (William Shatner) was the guest celebrity, and I thought it odd that a starship captain was hunting grizzlies in Alaska—on earth instead of Taurus IV or some such planet light years away.

George Bird Evans—actually his wife, Kay—was one of the first to shoot grouse and woodcock video back in the sixties. In *The Upland Shooting Life*, he writes of doing so in the first few pages of the book. "But mostly it is just Kay with her movie camera and I with my gun and the setters, saturating ourselves with experiences that feed the soul," he wrote. There's a full-page photo of the couple later in the book, George with his side-by-side and Kay holding both her video camera and what looks like a pheasant. It's clear that "saturating [himself] with experience" meant he was holding a shotgun in his hands and not a camera. Kay's filming recorded for posterity the lives of his Old Hemlock setters and the upland way of life, a video still available from the Old Hemlock Foundation.

One of the problems with hunting media, in particular video, however, is its diminishment and distortion of the reality in the field. For sure, sports writing and images (photography, drawings, and paintings) reflect the perspective of the writer, photographer, and artist, who alter reality to suit their artistic vision. For example, I rarely see wildlife art depicting nasty weather or the times when game is scarce. We want our grouse to flush by the dozens in the clear, which is only natural because this is one of our recurring dreams, or at least it's one of mine.

Reality, in my experience, is quite different, as any grouse hunter who has walked all day and flushed one or two birds in the cold rain knows, particularly if the one and only grouse you saw all day flushed as you were trying to limbo under a fallen tree. Grouse and woodcock hunting can be hard work, which is also what makes it so rewarding. It requires time, practice, patience, physical effort, and sometimes a little suffering, none of which films well.

One would think film would be more honest, as it records exactly what happened at that moment. Yet video distorts time critically, altering the reality of hunting by what it leaves out. For instance, a video of grouse hunting would never show the forty-five-minute walk necessary to reach a favored covert. If it did, no one would watch beyond the first minute. On the typical thirty-minute white-tail video, we can witness dozens of record-book bucks get shot or arrowed, more than most seasoned hunters could possibly see in their hunting lifetimes, much less kill. We also get a rock-and-roll soundtrack and lots of backslapping. Focusing on kills compresses years of hunting and acquiring the essential skills into just a few moments, shortcutting the craft and process. If this is what kids and inexperienced hunters expect (a limit of birds or a twelve-point buck on every outing), the real-world scarcity of wild game might frighten them all the way back to their basements for more screen time.

Scarcity of game is one of the constraints of the natural world that video can sidestep and alter through editing. (How much film time is recorded for a typical whitetail video?) I can remember only a handful of times when grouse and woodcock were so thick it seemed as if I were the hero of a hunting video, and all but two of those times were during the woodcock flight. I've experienced far more days when I flushed one or two ruffed grouse, a bird for every hour of walking, an experience that would never make it to video. Recording the kill is primary when it comes to film. Film does a much poorer job of recording the more subtle, and perhaps more important, aspects of the hunt. And ultimately, these more subtle aspects are not what we watch hunting videos for.

In this sense, real boots-on-the-ground hunting seems pretty dull compared with the virtual form. But only in a two-dimensional sense, for grouse and woodcock hunting in the woods is infinitely richer, so much more that words and images can never fully capture the spirit and feel of a real hunt. You literally have to be there.

I'll admit to being an old curmudgeon who has never been seduced by screens or the idea that a sweep of our fingers can change reality. I was raised in a different era and, growing up, didn't have to face the video temptations of today. Our family had three channels when they all came in.

Instead, I spent my autumns exploring the hills of northeastern Iowa, hunting squirrels, rabbits, and the occasional pheasant. If I had to choose between hunting and *The American Sportsman*, I was out the door roaming the woods and fields. So it's easy for me to criticize hunting videos when as a kid I never had to deal with their enticements or face the addiction they pose. Who knows how different I would be today if I had spent the majority of my free time in my bedroom watching video instead of outdoors "saturating myself with experience."

No matter the medium through which we experience hunting, however, it will inevitably diminish its essence. As a writer, I fully understand this, knowing my words invariably fall well short of really capturing a grouse or woodcock hunt. Sometimes words come close to evoking the experience, but more often than not, they seem woefully wide of the mark, flat on the paper, inadequate. How does one put into words the intensity of the flush or the point, the single-mindedness of a good bird dog charging through the woods, the way the wispy clouds look like setter tails in the October blue sky, the good and familiar ache in the knees at the end of a long day? The inadequacy of words doesn't keep me from reading or writing; I just never choose to do so when I have the opportunity to hunt. And I hope you feel the same way, experiencing directly the joys of the hunt through your own five senses and not just two-dimensionally through the eyes.

Edward O. Wilson claimed in his book *Biophilia* that we have an "innate tendency to focus on life and lifelike processes," and humans are drawn toward life like moths to a light. In other words, we desire and are fulfilled by the natural world, just as we desire and are fulfilled by good food. As more and more of us live in cities and urban areas and move away from the countryside, and as technology increasingly shields us from nature, we connect less and less with the natural world. Some researchers and writers (see Richard Louv's *Last Child in the Woods*) go so far as to say that most Americans experience a nature-deficit disorder, which, they claim, might be the root of many behavioral problems.

Grouse hunting will probably never be prescribed as a cure for nature-deficit disorder, nor would insurance companies pay out for this kind of therapy whenever we feel depressed or suicidal. With school shootings commonplace nowadays, no school board would use grouse and woodcock hunting as an antidote to nature-deficit disorder. It's up to the elders in the hunting community to pass on and preserve the remedy.

If our only connection to the natural world and hunting is mediated, then that world is greatly diminished. Nothing beats the real thing, the heft and warmth of a grouse in hand, the last popple leaves of the season twirling down to earth, the smell of autumn, the tinkling of the dog's bell working toward the tag alders down along the creek.

And if you have made it to the end of this essay, put down this book and *go hunt*!

Home Covert

This covert starts at home, from the front door of our cabin on land we bought twenty-five years ago. We own about eight acres total, basically a woodlot, but thousands of acres of county forest surround our place, so much land we could never really begin to know all its secrets. When we bought the land, the previous owner told us our woods was once pasture, providing fodder for a few of the thousands of horses once necessary in northern Wisconsin to log the vast pineries. This is why, he said, grass still grows beneath the northern red oaks and sugar maples, the oaks a uniform eighty to ninety years old. Having cut several red oaks for firewood and counted the rings, I know this.

In April and May, wildflowers bloom beneath the leafless trees—hepatica, bloodroot, trout lilies, and, in a few secret places, the chance lady's slipper—the flowers of the forest. This intense blooming before the canopy steals the sun culminates with the trillium, thousands of white flowers strewn around our woods as if a giant had spilled his popcorn there.

Since our woods is mature and so open we could drive a truck around most of it, the cover is not suitable for much wild game. The deer only pass through as does the random bear, on occasion trailed by hounds. Down the road in a field not much larger than a city lot, male woodcock sing and sky-dance in spring. A small patch of popple sits in the northeast corner of our land, and years ago a grouse drummed there in September, often in dark of night, but I could never find his drumming log.

Before we built our cabin, we were camping on the edge of our property, on ground that is now our driveway. After two days of camping with our two grouse dogs coursing all over the property, we discovered a hen grouse nesting about ten yards from where we had pitched the tent. She had picked an ideal nesting location backed up to an old rotting stump in a clump of brush. I was stomping around, looking for a potential site for our future cabin, when I spotted her dark eye. Then the rest of her body materialized out of the gray and dun colors of the spring forest. I backed away slowly and returned with a disposable camera for a few shots. We packed up shortly thereafter, keeping an eye on the dogs, and left the hen in peace. When we returned a few weeks later she and her chicks, the eggs shells scattered about the stump, had moved on. We wished them luck.

Being so close to us, I have no idea why or how the dogs never smelled her, unless she put out little scent because she barely moved a feather those two days. When we left our campsite with the dogs for a walk or a longer mountain bike ride, did she jump up off her nest and forage for bugs and whatnot, hustling back to the still warm eggs cupped in her nest before we returned with the dogs?

Other than those chance encounters, however, ruffed grouse on our land have been understandably scarce, but this changes once I walk to the east and wander into the county forest, which butts up against our property. The county has cut this land twice in the past twenty years, once thinning a red pine stand and the other time clearcutting an overmatured section of popple. Other than a few massive white pines, most of the cover to the east of us is immature and brushy—ideal bird cover.

When we arrive at our cabin during bird season, usually for a long weekend, my first hunt is invariably through the Home Covert, which is anywhere I can reach on foot from the front door. In late August and early September, before either the grouse or woodcock season has opened, we head out in the early morning in search of woodcock scattered about, before the heat or the mosquitoes or the ticks—perhaps a combination thereof—drive us out of the woods and back to the cabin.

Instead of a shotgun, preseason I carry a camera, hoping for a shot or two despite the heavy foliage and the darkness under the canopy. But taking a photograph is not like taking a shot. Taking a picture is capturing an image, an idea; it's philosophical in its way. Hunting is a committed action with deadly intent. As I've said, I wish there were some form of shoot and release, but only on certain occasions at certain times. Most of the season, I pull the trigger knowing absolutely that a well-placed shot string could end the life of a grouse or a woodcock. This intent changes me from philosopher of nature to participant in nature. Like José Ortega y Gasset, I believe one must kill in order to have hunted.

In the modern world, we spend most of our time outside nature and not in it, in a world of our own fashioning. We spend our days within cars and four walls. We constantly look at screens. I feel this acutely when I ride my bicycle home from work in the city. I leave the heart of the city and pedal past the ever-creeping development. This world is composed of asphalt, concrete, and steel, the noise of the traffic deafening. Passing under the interstate, the roar of traffic overhead rumbling on the bridge, I pedal past a vast health-care and insurance campus. Here are manicured lawns, exotic trees, and nonindigenous flowers in neat planters, along with machines in the garden—the mowers, weed whackers, leaf blowers, and sprayers necessary for complete control.

After chugging up the hill and over the final ridge, I start to feel the city fall away. Our everyday home is on the edge of the city, nestled up next to the woods, so we have had bear, deer, turkey, fox, and coyote—not to mention the legions of smaller species like whitethroats and grosbeaks—wander through and, on occasion, live on our one acre. The city still hums away down the hill, but we have moved away to some degree from the human-dominated environment.

Like this move away from the bustle of city life, hunting puts me even deeper into nature, at times giving me what Ortega y Gasset called a "vacation from the human condition." The human condition I'm trying to escape are the constructs we've forged over the millennia, including the concept of time itself. I don't like to wear a watch while hunting because it often reminds me I need to be somewhere else in a few hours. If this sounds as if I'm advocating a return to a more animallike existence, I suppose I might be, but isn't that the goal of outdoor recreation—to re-create those older conditions and the primitive life of our forebears? Hunting and, on occasion, fishing haul me back to that primitive state.

When I leave our cabin during hunting season, I typically head east down our trail, turning right at a No ATVs sign on our property line. This trail through the county forest leads to other threads of trails—logging roads, fainter two-tracks, ski trails, and mountain bike singletrack—fanning out like a delta. These trails and pathways are human constructs, too, and we often take them, but the deer and wolves walk them as well. On these trails, you could hike straight north fifty miles to Lake Superior all on public land; it's one vast public commons, a gift to hunters and whoever else wants to use this land.

Jenkins always takes a hard left at the rock cairn marking the first trail, a mountain bike singletrack, for this is the usual turn for the exercise loop we walk, run, or ride in winter, spring, and summer. He dove around the corner and sprinted up the trail, before he realized I was not following and ran back with a questioning look on his face. "This way," I said and pointed east and continued on down the county trail. He jetted back and tore off past me down this trail, happy to be running somewhere, anywhere. We dropped downhill, and I scooted off the trail heading for a pothole to the south. These small depressions, called kettles, punctuate the landscape. They are natural amphitheaters left behind by the last glacier. When the ice blocks melted, these kettles formed. We have a shallow one that drops ten feet or so behind our cabin, and it's home to bloodroot and hepatica. A half mile to the north lies Norwegian Hollow, one of the largest and deepest kettles in the area. Northeast is Raccoon Hollow, where Ox, our first setter, once pointed a massive raccoon slumbering in the October sun. When it jumped up and ran off, it was so large we thought at first it was a wolf or a coyote.

On the north side of the trail lies a matching kettle. I should have names for all these landmarks, but I don't. The northern kettle hosts mostly older popple and red pine, but the kettle to the south is home to a thriving patch of popple recently cut, and on occasion it holds a bird or two. I stayed high up on the kettle rim and watched Jenkins work the popple down in the bottom, the tinkling of his bell drifting up to me. If he went on point, I would have to scoot down the hillside in that rough cover. As he worked the bottom of the bowl, a grouse ripped out of the popple ahead of him and fled to the east, up the rim and over the sand road I knew was there but couldn't see. It set its wings and glided into the cover on the other side. "Bird," I yelled down to Jenkins, who had a frozen front paw raised after picking up either the fresh scent or the flushing sound. "Be careful. There's birds in there," I scolded.

I hustled down toward him, thinking there might be another one or two grouse skulking in the popple. Jenkins, seeing me moving down the hillside, relaxed out of his point and worked forward, approaching the spot where the bird flushed. I tried to keep my feet underneath me to be ready for a shot, difficult on the cant of the hillside, in case of a wild flush. If it flew this way, I should get a good look at it.

Halfway down the kettle, I again halted and watched the dog work the scent, trying to piece together the bird-dog connection. He slowed and paused for a few seconds, hunkering down into a point, but then he released when he lost the scent, and I relaxed my grip on my shotgun. Jenkins worked up and out of the kettle, then circled around and back down toward me.

We scrambled up and out of the kettle, crossed the road, and then headed for another even more promising kettle lying farther to the east. This cover was actually the one I had in mind when we had set out. We bushwhacked, going cross-country. A few years back, we passed through near here, and I nearly kicked the neatly cleaned skull of a four-point buck, a trophy I slipped into my game bag. Back home, I hung it on the garage over the door.

Only in the fall while hunting—or occasionally in the spring when training or banding woodcock, another kind of hunting—do I forgo the smooth pathways we've created, the ruts we often find ourselves in. Only hunting takes me to places deep in the woods, usually on the heels of either Fergus or Jenkins, and doing so gives me a better understanding of my surroundings and my place in it. Others may employ different ways to understand their home country, and many no doubt have a greater understanding of their place, but for me, following a grouse dog through the woods is how the country best reveals itself to me. Behind them, I just might learn something.

And Jenkins was leading me to one such place now, a low, wet seep bordered by tag alders on one side and tamarack on the other. A few of the tamaracks had turned golden, our only coniferous tree that tries to compete with the maples. This seep was likely the hiding place for a second bird we wild-flushed just a few minutes earlier. That bird was loafing on the side of the trail and surprised us both. Over the years, we've gotten up a lot of birds in this place we're approaching, and as I made my way down over a low ridge, Jenkins was working the edge of the tags. He knew most likely the wild-flushed bird had dropped in there. Perhaps the first one we flushed was hunkered down there as well.

He started to slow, a sign he is making game. Then he hunkered down and crept forward, until his self-restraint overrode his prey drive and he pointed with right rear leg lifted and held in a position that looked like he was not quite sure where he should put it down. It was time for me to take over, and I hurried up past Jenkins, ready for an explosion of grouse out of the brush ahead. But the bird had other ideas—refusing to submit to the narrative written in my head—and blew out behind us, and as I wheeled around at the sound, it barreled through a dense screen of balsam fir and older popple, escaping a second time.

We followed, both of us well keyed up now. Jenkins seemed to want the bird more than I did. It took little time for Jenkins to make game again. *Surely the bird flew deeper than this into the balsams.* Jenkins didn't seem to think so, locking down again in a point, and I came in from his left.

The bird, for once, thundered up just about where I thought it would, according to Jenkins's head angle and body position. Thoreau wrote that "heaven is under our feet as well as over our heads," and just like the May trilliums or December snow, the ruffed grouse underfoot was heavenly, even if it sent a searing jolt through me, up my legs, and out the top of my head. It flushed right to left, and I swiped at it with my shotgun, pulled the trigger, and the bird tumbled, falling down a steep slope on the backside of the balsams.

This time everything had worked right for us, my narrative matching reality. It was fairly open woods, like that of so many grouse paintings, so Jenkins found the bird shortly, and I quickly grabbed it from him before he mauled it with his hard mouth. It was a nice mature gray bird, not like the smaller birds I had been shooting in the early part of the season. We turned for home, after Jenkins whiffed the still warm and fragrant body one more time, and I eased it into my game bag. I wished my dogs could talk and tell me what grouse and woodcock smell like.

One was enough for today. One was enough for most days, but I especially didn't want to overshoot the birds close to home, even though this is public ground. An ATV trail runs nearby, offering easy access to a crowd known for not wasting shells on flying birds. There's no law against any licensed small-game hunter coming through here and taking a legal limit of five birds. Even though I considered the birds to be my neighbors, I was still possessive of them, thinking them "mine." Living close by, I have conferred to myself some sort of ownership title, which was wrong as well as foolish. When I see the scattered feathers of where a grouse has been killed in the neighborhood, an irrational jealousy burns through me. *How dare that owl or goshawk or ATVer take* my *bird.*

Back home, Fergus was squealing behind the front door, upset over being left behind. From the cabin, he watched us walk away down the trail. Bitterly jealous, he desperately wanted to smell where we had been, what we had been doing. Before hanging the bird by the front door, I let him bury his nose for a snort of the coffee-flecked breast feathers, while Jenkins flopped down on his side in the grass, exhausted from his work.

Inside the house, I made a cup of coffee, then came back outside to sit on the front stoop with the dogs. The Home Covert radiates out from our front door. There is too much of it to know in several lifetimes, and I am continually surprised to discover something new here—a black bear den, a seep where skunk cabbage grows, a patch of wild leeks—just minutes from our front door. I can never know it all.

Friends constantly tell us we need to travel more, one even suggesting a canned Caribbean cruise. I tell them there are so many places I want to go in my neighborhood, let alone Wisconsin, the Midwest, or the rest of the country. Then there's Canada and Alaska. Hunting friends propose we hunt quail in Kansas or blue grouse in Montana, and we would love to do so, but there's all this around here, not to mention the next county over. There's so much to see and know right here.

As I drained my coffee cup, I recounted some of the birds I had shot in past Octobers and Novembers in the Home Covert, and a few on September's opening morning when the humid woods were dense with summer's load of vegetation. Inside the cabin, some of the tail fans of these birds grace our shelves, keepsakes of memorable hunts.

Grouse and woodcock connect me to this place. (Susan Parman)

It *is* the grouse and woodcock that connect me to this place, all the more so since their flesh and blood have joined mine. They are the true natives of this place, the heart of its wildness, and their flesh and blood impart a bit of their spirit to me and bind me to this place. They bring me home.

Acknowledgments

For careful reading of and valuable editorial suggestions about my manuscript, thanks to Dennis LaBare and Susan Parman.